MELODIES OF HUMANITY:

THE GOLDEN KEYS

"Humans who awaken themselves with benevolence, also become selfless and empower themselves with the melodies of humanity."

Ann Marie Ruby

Disclaimer:

This book ("*Melodies Of Humanity: The Golden Keys*") only represents the personal views of the author. In no way, does it represent or endorse any religious, philosophical, political, or scientific view. It has been written in good faith for people of all cultures and beliefs. Any resemblance to actual persons, living or dead, is purely coincidental. This book has been written in American English.

Published in the United States of America, 2023.

ISBN-13: 979-8-9875085-4-1

DEDICATION

"I awakened my soul through the sweet words of poetry. Now, I give you my gift of poetry to awaken yours."

Sweet words, or are they harsh? Are they painful and at times are they forewarning signs? Yet placed in a poem, they talk to me. Poetry for me is an emotional journey through one's consciousness. Poetry is timeless and a bridge between generations. What you the young shall recite tonight with your beloved, will through the gap of time be recited by your grandchildren with their beloveds. Maybe you will awaken some young generations to believe in themselves and awaken their society to accept one another through the sweet words of poetry.

Poems retell stories about situations and certain experiences. They hold on to the tears of a soul and let all who read them catch a drop of these tears through the dried ink on the paper. They are at times love stories, yet at times they are tragic stories that had started but never ended.

Throughout time though, all authors have tried to write about social awareness through short stories, novels, and poetry. They touch our inner mind, body, and soul more than we can ever express through words. The funny thing is all of these poems are written through simple words. Yet if we try to express our feelings, our throat finds itself caught in a wordless zone. The words that are in our heart just refuse to come out. That's when we appreciate poets and express our own feelings through their words.

My poetry book *Love Letters: The Timeless Treasure* is a book I had to write for myself. I had written my love letters in poetry format for my twin flame in hope that one day maybe he will find them. Yet I send my letters out to all of you as I bound them in a book, so you all can recite them with your beloved. I know you too want to recite them with your beloved or maybe through these touching endless treasures, you will awaken yourself and find your twin flame.

My books *Spiritual Songs: Letters From My Chest* and *Spiritual Songs II: Blessings From A Sacred Soul* were written to unite people from all different faiths. They are books you can open and recite with all race, color, and religion.

In this book of poetry, I have selected social awareness as my guide for I believe words are the only door which unites humanity with humans. My words are my bridge to the inner soul of all humans. Through words I will manifest humanity to spread from one soul to all the others. Nothing can stop this as I believe the power of the mighty pen is greater than anything in this world.

Each poem is a story, a song of a person who wants our one world to unite for humanity. I know you too believe humanity is before anything, any hatred, or any differences.

For where and when humanity is questioned, we the humans unite and show the world in its inner soul, there still are humans with humanity. Love is always the winner when division is questioned. We would rather stand together than divide ourselves. When we stand together, shoulder-to-shoulder, no division can enter through the gap that is invisible.

For the most powerful human trait humanity, I have written this book of poetry I call, *Melodies Of Humanity: The Golden Keys*. For my love for humans and my belief in humanity, I dedicate this book not to an individual person but to all humans with humanity.

TABLE OF CONTENTS

Others

INTRODUCTION

"Educate yourself to better the society, not to be an individual standing above all but to be amongst all."

The intolerance, the unawareness, and the detachment we have amongst ourselves will take down our society for these will never unite or grow our society. Today, our generation has amongst us highly educated humans, yet I believe they have left the main course of education far behind while they moved on. How could all your education make any difference to the society if you alienate the society from yourself by declaring yourself above all?

Science has advanced, education has advanced, yet the society has moved backward. I wonder if we are all getting educated to better ourselves and the society around us, then where have we gone wrong? Why are we standing by the shore and not waiting for dawn to arrive and warn all of the upcoming dangers of the sea? Why is it we leave everyone else in the dark when we get ourselves educated and stand above all, not with all?

The song has become too common as I hear all around me, "It's not your problem" or "Let it be and just move on." When I see the children who are left behind in the park to play by themselves because of their skin color, their religious differences, or social status, I break down in tears. Yes, I too walk away in silence as I fear the parents arguing with me, or the neighbors saying it's not my problem.

Every day I wonder if I could do anything to awaken humanity within at least one human, or maybe a group of people. I shall not shelter my fears within my inner soul, but I will bring out the most powerful tool God has given us, the pen. All the words I can't say to all, I can write down with my pen. I remember my third-grade teacher in Australia had told my class to write down our feelings and he would read them and decide if we were all doing all right or had any problems.

I will open the doors to all the problems as I can't close them and let them be a prisoner in my chest. I will through my key, the pen, write out the obstacles of this society I see through my inner eyes on my papers. Then, I will bind my papers in a book and have them sent out to all who will have them. Maybe one at a time, you will find my words and acknowledge the problems.

Life is a blessed journey and it's a blessing when there are no hurdles ahead of us. If there are hurdles, it's better to know where, when, and why they are there, so we can avoid this route. My words are a guide to your inner hearts. Let's not be the divider, but let's be the unifier.

How would all of this education benefit anyone if you stand alone gloating about your achievements to all, which happens to divide all? Even a king of the land is only successful when all of his subjects love him and say he too walks amongst us, like us. A leader is only successful and will only be a leader when his countrymen walk with him, not against him.

A human too can be successful if people listen to him. Yet I know within the loud wrongful voices, the quiet and rightful voices get drained out. It is then we follow the wrong, not the right. So, I say it is not the leader or the king who is powerful, but you who follow him.

I will be amongst the humans who silently stand for the right. Yet I won't be silent as I will be loud through the most powerful instruments humans have. Yes, I, the speaker of truth, shall not be fearful. I shall not be loud nor graceless. I will use my pen and the dried ink of my pen will become louder than all the wrong and shall eventually unite humans with their lost humanity. For remember, you have not lost your humanity. It's just misplaced as you are indoctrinated by the wrong.

Through the pages of this book of poetry, I have tried to write down my words in a poetry format. I hope all of you by accepting my book will give me strength to spread this simple word of humanity throughout our one world with love, tenderness, and kindness.

After years of meditation and trying to find a solution to end all the crises on this Earth, I realized they all have one answer, humanity. The world needs to awaken through humanity. The golden key that will open the door to humanity and resolve all of our troubles is you the individual as within your heart, you carry the core message of humanity which is love and understanding. Yes, it's not the world leaders, nor is it the law enforcement organization, nor is it your billionaire neighbors, for it's you the individual.

I have searched far and near as to what I could do to be of help to this world. I have awakened my inner soul through humanity. I see the world as one home and the world population, all race, color, and religion as my one human family. I realized I could help by awakening your inner souls through humanity.

Just think if you awaken yourself. Then through your kindness, you could spread humanity to our human brothers and sisters, one by one. We would see our human family, the greatest creation on Earth, are all walking for humanity by awakening themselves first as they realized in their own chest they carry the golden key we all call benevolence. This one world would only then become a safe, secure, prosperous, peaceful, and a happy home.

So all the humanitarian crises I have mentioned in this book would be resolved slowly through you the individual being aware and awakening within humanity. I realized I could not travel far or beyond to get my message out, nor could I knock on all doors to spread my message of humanity. So, I picked up my blessed pen and wrote poetry. These poems are not a lecture from a politician, nor a warning from a law enforcement official. These are timeless treasures from a friend.

I know when all things fail and nothing touches the human soul, it is then the sweet words of a poet can awaken all as they leave a permanent seal within the chests of the readers. I hope my poetry awakens you the individual. As all individuals awaken themselves within humanity, this one world will only then become our safe haven. After reading these poems, I know you too will be a part of the solution, not a part of the problem.

I have named this book *Melodies Of Humanity: The Golden Keys* as I believe all humans around the globe will awaken with these melodies. For this one world to be our one safe haven, you the individual must open your eyes to these humanitarian crises. Let's all in union recite these poems to all humans across the globe. We can catch all humans with poetry, not with anger, so let's melodiously solve the world humanitarian crises. The subtitle is the *Golden Keys* as each individual has within their inner chest a golden key he or she can use to open and become a part of the solution. The solution will only happen through your love and care for your human family, the human race, through the golden key which is your selfless love.

As dawn comes upon my door, I hear the melodies of the visiting birds singing. They tell me songs still exist as the amazing sun kisses my head and reminds me another day has arrived upon my door with new hope for the day. If in the skies huge clouds are floating, I appreciate the amazing clouds for giving me privacy. The pouring rains that appear on my land are pouring love for this world as they make my world greener and fill my garden with beautiful colorful flowers.

I know the harmony of this world is not missing. It just got silent through the loud powerful voices of the blistering unjust mouths. The loud, scary, and thunderous voices have taken over the world. Yet the artist, the author, the cinema maker, and the melodious singer are still out there. They are quietly trying to make our world a better and kinder place to live in. I too have joined them and through my pen, I have written my melodies. I hope you will find them and spread harmonious melodies from this book around our world.

This book is written against bigotry, division, and ignorance that bring down our society. I write for love and coalition between humans and societies that will keep our one world strong and growing. I can only write my poems but I need you to spread them for you are the melodious, harmonious, and fearless soul whom my book of poetry seeks.

May my melodies find you as I found the courage to write them. Now you too can spread humanity around the globe as you awaken yourself first. Let's unite and stand on a bridge of harmony together, you and I, through the pages of this treasure chest I call, *Melodies Of Humanity: The Golden Keys*.

POEM ONE:

A SOCIETY'S DESTINY IS HUMANITY

"Destiny is absent in a society without humanity."

A SOCIETY'S DESTINY IS HUMANITY

Lost and stranded, in confusion,

Walking backward, and in circles,

Are the twenty-first century's

Civilized societies as

They stop to ask one another

For directions while they journey

Across time with the lost feelings.

"Did we forget something?" they ask.

"Did we leave anything behind?"

They knock upon doors to inquire.

"Maybe we'll find what is missing

Ahead of us as we're seeking."

The journey only goes forward.

They have to stop and they must think,

"What could be missing from our lives?"

They realize they can't go back to the past,

And they can't go to the future

For the answers of what they have lost.

Then the twenty-first century's humans

Think,

How will they find their destination,

If they don't know what they have lost,
Or left behind?
They know they have walked backward,
Far more than even their ancestors,
As no one before had thought
They lost their destination
As they did not even know their destiny.
Could they take refuge somewhere,
Maybe in a broken system,
Where all the people
Walk lost and stranded,
Where nothing is found as
How could one
Find shelter
In the lost and confused world?
The civil societies all
Seek the perfect destination.
For guidance they stand
By the shore of the past
As the musical
Lessons of the past
Come sweeping like a
Morning breeze,
As the past sings a tune

And reminds the present society,

To beware where they have lost

Their destiny.

For the humans of this century must

Remember

They cannot travel to the past,

Nor can they travel

To the future,

But only be in the present,

To ask, seek, and knock

Upon

The missing path of life.

For all to cross time and

Be in the future

With dignity, grace, and courage,

They must know

Their eventual destiny.

For a society will succeed together

If they all recognize

Like their ancestors did,

And their descendants

Will remember

From their guidance,

A SOCIETY'S DESTINY IS HUMANITY.

SOCIETY'S DESTINY:

We the humans of the twenty-first century must make ourselves aware of our basic human values. These values make us love ourselves and self-respect is found within the eyes of I, the individual.

Now across the world, we are facing humans who have lost their humanity. They are lacking self-recognition through their own eyes. I ask everyone to stop and look at your own image in the mirror of your inner soul. Now find your true self and pick up your basic human values. The values you have left behind, keep them in your inner chest and send them to your future generations as the golden keys of their lives.

These messenger keys will forever open their treasure boxes. For only then will our future generations too find humanity within themselves which we have from our journey through life given them as lessons of life. When they hold on to these lessons, they too will know and teach their future generations, a society's destiny is humanity.

POEM TWO:

HUMANITY IS WHEN YOU ARE HUMANE

"Humans can't survive where there is no humanity, so be humane and survive with one another through humanity."

HUMANITY IS WHEN YOU ARE HUMANE

The greatest of all beings

Are the human beings,

Yet what about the humans

Is so great,

I ask?

Is it your capacity

To control all other beings?

Or is it the capacity to

Rule the Earth?

Maybe it is the power of

Knowing humans are above all.

Then do you call yourselves

Greater than one another too?

Where do you,

Or when do you

Stop calling yourselves the

Supreme power,

Or the greatest of all?

Are all humans the greatest?

Are all humans recognized

For being the best of all

Beings?

For what traits do you or any one

Other human

Have to be considered the greatest?

For it is understood,

Humans with humanity are the

Greatest beings on Earth.

It is humanity that separates a human from being

The best or the worst,

Amongst all humans?

The answer found within all humans

With humanity,

Defines the unanswered questions

For all across the world.

For humanity defines

The human beings as

The greatest on Earth

As it separates

The man from the beast,

Yet do remember,

Not all humans

Have humanity,

For

HUMANITY IS WHEN YOU ARE HUMANE.

HUMANITY:

The Earth today is ruled by the humans who have left behind their humane selves. I wander around the globe for one humanitarian soul. With the extinction of the dinosaurs, we had become the greatest living beings on Earth. I wonder have our humane behaviors become extinct?

We all depend on scientific proofs and social acceptance before we make up our minds. We follow our chosen political, religious, and even cultural groups. It matters not who or what path we follow if we keep humanity within our souls. So today, as you go out and start your day, remember, you the one who calls yourself the greatest being on Earth, to walk with humanity as you pick up your humane characteristics.

Questions and answers are crowding the air as all ask what humanity is. How could you say or know who a humanitarian is or not? I don't have the answer for that, but in my mind it is simple. Humanity is when you are humane.

POEM THREE:

NEVER BEND BEFORE UNJUST

"Don't bend and twist to make yourself fit in with the wrong, for then you will never get yourself back from the unjust and become part of the failed justice system."

NEVER BEND BEFORE UNJUST

Roaming around the society,

Trying to fit in,

Searching for a friend,

Even if the friend

Is not a person

With inherent basic

Moral values.

Always trying to watch out

For those who are

Keeping an eye on you,

Watching if you have

Walked out of the line,

Your newly-found group

Is following you.

They know what you are saying.

They know what you are doing.

They watch if where you

Live gets their approval.

They won't approve of your

Older friends.

They won't accept your own

Desires,

Or your rejections,

For they will decide of your

Needs and yours not,

As they will make

You bend toward them.

They will

Make you do and speak

As they control you.

For if you don't have a will,

And only pick a friend or a group

To be noticed

By the rejecters,

You will not be seen

By them

Or anyone else

As you will then

Become the invisible.

For you are not a mannequin,

They can bend and adjust

As they will,

And as they please.

You are a human with

Your own mind,

Your own body,

And your own soul,

So be your own self.

Be on the right

Side of history

And remember to

NEVER BEND BEFORE UNJUST.

JUSTICE SYSTEM:

Don't become part of the failed justice system. Don't follow any leader or a group to become the unjust. I ask you, do you say only what the others want to hear? Or do you keep your emotions buried to only please the others? That's the mantra followed by today's generation. Not because we are selfless but actually selfish. Because we want to fit in the group, not go against it. By doing so, we are hurting the truth.

Today on this Earth, we all try to please the others. Wrong they may be, yet our voices find no words and are lost within our thoughts before they can even make a sound. At times, we stay quiet in fear of offending the others, even though the others are inhumane. Yet what about you, your voice, your feelings, and your own dignified self-conscience?

Don't be the lost voices of the society. Speak up and be your own friend if no one else wants to be your friend. Yet don't be a friend of the wrong and give them more power as you lose your own self and lose to give the power to the right. When we lose electricity or power, we are forced to be in the dark. Why are you being forced to be in the dark when all you need to do is stand up with a candle in your hands?

Remember when you wake up with dawn tomorrow, as you become courageous and are able walk out of the dark night, be the change and have some self-respect for yourself. Don't look at yourself down the path of time gone by and lose all of yourself and your self-respect. Everything might be lost but don't lose your consciousness. You will face time and will be questioned about your involvement in making the society lose its self-respect and making today's society the unjust society of all times.

Ask yourself today, how will you retell losing all self-respect to your future generation? Change today as today you still have time, for tomorrow it will be a lost chance. Let the justice system remain impartial. Walk for and with the just. Never bend before unjust.

POEM FOUR:

CELEBRATE DIVERSITY

"The skies, the Earth, and the sea celebrate their differences in a portrait eternally. Let the human eyes learn from this picture-perfect sketch and celebrate diversity."

CELEBRATE DIVERSITY

The skies, the Earth,

And the sea,

Blend within one another

Phenomenally.

The moon awakens

Within the chest of the skies

As she pours her glory,

Upon the Earth and the sea,

Creating a glowing harmony.

Yet I ask myself,

Why can't we the humans,

Blend in harmoniously

Within one blessed family,

Where we would rejoice

The differences?

We would be framed,

Like a perfect portrait,

Hanging on the wall

To be loved,

And be admired

Throughout time

By one and by all.

As we cross over in
The wagon of time,
These social, religious,
And racial
Differences would be
Celebrated as our
Human footprints,
Eternally.
The future would
Rejoice and celebrate,
As they read
The historical
Paths created by
The different footprints
Of their human ancestors.
Each page would have
Different stories retold,
Left behind
On the fallen leaves
By the past ancestors.
The future descendants
Would find colorful
Portrayals left behind by
Different sizes, different colors,

Different human races
To be framed in books,
And kept sacredly
Within the libraries
Of eternal life stories.
The flowing rivers,
The floating clouds,
And the fallen leaves
Would all in union
Write the human stories
Of how we like the skies,
The Earth,
And the sea,
Also
CELEBRATE DIVERSITY.

DIVERSITY:

Being different from your neighbor brings more diversity to the family of humans. The fact is we are a diverse group of humans living all across the world. Together we make an amazing portrait the Creator so gently sat and created with love. Individually we are unique, yet unitedly we are all the blessed human race.

Today, pick up your painter's brush and tray, and paint your human family from the seven continents of this one world. Frame your world family in a canvas keeping the Earth, the sea, and the skies in the background. This amazing picture you can proudly frame as a proof of your Creator's amazing creation.

Be the different and celebrate all differences as it is the greatest artist we all call our Creator who created this loving portrait of humans. Stand up and in union let all of us with optimism celebrate this happiness. The picture-perfect world our Creator created is different and makes our human family amazing. Maybe today we can appreciate all the children of this world as we celebrate diversity.

POEM FIVE:

STAND UP EVEN ALONE

"Alone and lonely, I walk like a stranger within your eyes, yet within my eyes, I am standing up against all kinds of discrimination."

STAND UP EVEN ALONE

I am left all alone,
As members of my society
Laugh at me.
They call me names.
My friends have alienated
Themselves,
For they don't want to
Acknowledge of
Ever being with me.
For I don't feel neglected,
I don't feel
Lonely,
Nor do I feel lost,
Or stranded,
For I know,
It is all right to be
Alienated.
It is just okay
To be left alone,
For it is comforting,
To know
No one can push

Or pull me
To do the wrong
For I walk for the right.
I stand with no one,
If all are walking for the wrong.
I shall go on my separate path
From you and all
Members of the society,
When I know it is
By choice you are alienating
One person, one group,
Or one creed,
Because they don't match your
Choice of life.
For it is then
I shall walk alone
For when our paths separate
I know it is then I have
Done the right thing,
For I stand on
The ground of
What is right,
As you stand on the ground of
All that is wrong.

On this path I have with me,

My inner conscience

As my best friend.

I will with my best friend's

Guidance,

STAND UP EVEN ALONE.

DISCRIMINATION:

All types of discrimination are a big step backward for our society. It's like we have all moved backward in time, as if we have not learned anything from history. Our forefathers have left us with their footsteps. We could study and learn from their mistakes and pick up the ways of their success.

In the past, we learned from Mahatma Gandhi who had from the past sent us his message of peace. We could have seen Martin Luther King, Jr., had walked a hard walk for the right course, even though at his time it was fatal. You could see your forefathers too had fought to unite people, not divide the society. Our teachers had told us to stand up for the right, even if that meant you would be the unpopular person in the room.

Today I watch young children walk to the lonely child on the school grounds and ask if he or she would like to be a friend or have a friend. Yet we the adults have walked away from each other. People have started to outright lie and make their blistered lies the truth by repeating the lie over and over again.

Do these repeated lies then become the truth just to be in the popular group, or does a lie always stay a lie? Is there one person amongst all of you who will walk to your own friend and group and say the simple word "No," you will not be a part of the lie, the wrong? Will you be able to stand up for the truth against your family, your friends, and your society?

Maybe you don't have the courage to be the brave in fear of retaliation. Perhaps one of you could be fearless and start a new group where no one lies, no one pretends to be a friend, where you won't find the fake laughs. Yet you will hear and listen to the truth even if it hurts. You will find open-hearted laughs fill your inner world. There, you all would find me.

I do hope to find some of you there. For I believe in that group, I will find my happy place. I won't stand up with any racial, religious, or ethnic bigotries of any kind. I will for you and for my own self-respect stand up even alone.

POEM SIX:

WALK AWAY FOR PEACE

"Marriages are made out of promises. Yet letting go of you is not my rejection of you but letting you know our promises were broken and have landed us apart on the divorce track. So, I walk away for peace."

WALK AWAY FOR PEACE

Love binds souls.

Love holds on to differences

Through a wagon

Of understanding.

Love is a two-way street.

Yet at times

When the two-way path

Gets separated

Through an ocean of differences,

It is then you

The one trying

To hold on to

Your love

For the both of you,

Must know when to let go.

For if you hold on

To a bridge made out of rope

Too tight,

The bridge you

Are trying to protect

Will tear.

If you let

The bridge made out of rope

Get too unfastened,

It will collapse.

The love

You once cherished,

The love you held in your inner

Soul so gently,

Now has gotten off

The railroad track.

So, it is time

For the better of your soul,

And the better of all

Other innocent souls,

You should now

WALK AWAY FOR PEACE.

DIVORCE:

Divorce is the curse word no one wants to talk about or touch. It's like another untouchable issue. In all relationships, people try to be understanding and at times, make it through, day by day. At times, we get in a relationship faster than we could say I do. Yet I ask what happens when all of the stories don't have happy endings? It's better than no stories being told at all. All stories told today are lessons for tomorrow. So, it's better to be married and try to make it, and if the story ends before it's time, then it just wasn't meant to be.

People of today are trying to follow our past ancestors. We try to learn from our ancestors and try to follow their achievements and failures. Yet time and tide have washed away all the footprints on the sands left behind by our ancestors. We can only see our own footprints being created by us as we travel forward. Today, I watch some of you trying to make it through rough and tough times, which is admirable and well-deserving if it works out.

Some of you know it is a risk for you to be in a relationship. You don't know if you will even see the daylight tomorrow because of the risky and battered relationship or situation you have entered. This situation you have entered should never be punishable by asking you to stay on track and see if you will drown or survive after the heavy storm is over. Your train will get off track and let's hope no other innocent life is on board.

It's adventurous to sit on a boat and watch the storm through the dark night. Yet there is a great risk you and the boat you are trying to stay put in will not complete your dangerous adventure, and all involved in this situation will drown.

If only there was someone else holding on to you during the storm, whose hands you would hold on to, knowing you could survive through all dangerous storms for him or with him. If the storm is the person you wanted to hold on to, yet he has become the dark storm you are trying to escape or survive through or from, then let him go. It's at times better to just let go of the past and walk away for peace.

POEM SEVEN:

DEADLY SINS

"Lovers burning candles within one another tonight forget the passion at dawn might be the reason their candles of eternal love shall be eternally burnt for they have engaged in one night's deadly sins."

DEADLY SINS

The dark night's lethal attraction

Calls upon

The lovers

Blindfolded.

The passion, the heat, and the

Drunk minds can't think,

Can't breathe,

Can't even move

As they are both

Fused within

One another,

In a world of lust.

Is this love,

Or is this lust?

For within love you can think,

You can write songs.

You can sing

To one another.

You are the subject

Of the romantic

Poetry.

You are

The words of the

Romantic poet.

Yet here in the deadly night's

Passionate embrace,

You can't write poetry,

Or sing and listen to

The sweet songs

Of your beloved's

Heartbeats.

Yet you can only

Think of lust.

You can think of your selfish

Needs,

Of the one night's

Passionate

Dark kiss.

It's because you

Have spread your wings to

The vultures

To die within sin.

For after this night,

You will no longer fly

Like the nightingales,

Calling for your twin flame,

For you have burned

Yourself to ashes

Through one night's

Dark passionate embrace.

You will regret

Within your inner soul

At the first sight of dawn.

For then, you will only have spread

Your wings

To be infected,

With the deadly sins

Of the mortal bodies.

Eternally, you shall regret

And speak

To one and to all,

Through

The night skies,

And never enjoy love,

And never be the beloved

Of another,

But forever be the

One night's lover,

Who had spread

Your wings to die

In shame,

Not within the passionate

Embrace of

Your twin flame.

Your passionate

Embrace within the dark sin,

Eternally shall be

Known and called

Not as

True love,

Or as the union of true lovers,

But as the

One night's

DEADLY SINS.

DEADLY SINS:

Our forefathers and the scholars who had traveled upon the same path we travel upon had said, wait and be patient for everything comes to those who wait. They never finished their sentences to explain to us what happens to those who don't wait, who are impatient and fall prey to their own dark desires? It is a topic not discussed in a lot of societies as it's the mortal sin no one wants to talk about.

Those who have committed this, try to wake up and walk away from it when and if they realize their mistakes in time. Yet those of you jumping off your cautious wagons, do be careful and know you have been warned by me an unknown person for the dark diseases still exist which you will be infected by and then become the carrier as you spread them to others.

The unwanted pregnancies, the unwanted curses you will be the topic of shall never leave you alone. For I believe no pregnancies should be unwanted yet at times, it's you who must go through the shame and unwanted talks of life. If this relationship is incest, or maybe separating your best friend and their spouse, or just a dark side where you have entered willingly, remember this night's shame shall follow you like a shadow.

So my advice to you is wait and be patient. Love is to be cherished as it will come to your door. It will flow like the wind to your future generation through your patient waiting periods in due time. So tonight, if you are lonely, dream a little about your future, and at all costs avoid the one night's deadly sins.

POEM EIGHT:

EYES OF THE OTHERS

"Wrong I am yet why do I see myself as the right, and all others are wrong? It's then I know I must see myself through the eyes of the others."

ANN MARIE RUBY

EYES OF THE OTHERS

When I say something,

Or do something,

It comes out as

Wrong.

I know I tried my best,

Yet my words became

The pain,

The sufferings

For the

Others.

When I don't say something,

Then it is that

I am rude

And I am again wrong.

So, how is it

I too could be heard,

And seen

Without being

Rude,

Or

Mean and obnoxious?

For my inner heart too

Knows I was wrong,

Yet only after I

Had spoken.

My inner soul

Feels cold as I

Try to be nice but

My actions come out

As wrong,

Yet once again.

I stood in front of the mirror

To see my reflection,

Yet I only saw

My own eyes,

My own pain,

My own thoughts.

Then I stood

In front of

The one I hurt.

I watched her eyes.

I felt her inner soul.

I saw her tears

Falling

Because of my actions.

I realized my wrong,

My unkind words,

My unjust anger,

My pain

Had made

Another soul hurt

Another soul cry,

Another soul

Be in distress,

Which I could have

Prevented by

Not seeing myself,

My own reflection,

Or feeling

Not through my eyes

But through the

EYES OF THE OTHERS.

SEE THROUGH THE EYES OF THE OTHERS:

I have seen throughout this world we only see ourselves not the others. When I hurt or have a body ache, I can only think of my own pain. Then I see people walking around with much more pain and fear, yet they smile and make my day. I realized as a friend had said quite honestly, she gets scared when it's herself or her turn. Why is it we don't see the others?

It's so easy to cause pain to the people around us without even realizing. Someone had hurt me terribly when he had told me to place my book in his mail room and leave it there when I had it in my hands. He did not have the time to take the book as he was busy.

I left without giving it to him. He was shocked and asked, "You don't want me to have it or give it a read?" I realized he wanted to have it yet did not want to carry it himself. Or maybe he did not want people to know he had taken an unknown author's book. He was shocked and upset I had the courage to take my book back with me.

It's strange as people act according to their own feelings. I would want all of you to know simple words can be very painful and hurtful. You won't even realize what you have said or done until karma gives you a return envelope when the note says you got what you asked for. So, everyone don't say or do something you don't want to be said or done to you. I know if your fingers are cut, you have to take care of yourself. Yet when someone else's finger gets cut, do take time to notice and see if they are all right.

Just by acknowledging someone who has been there for you, you too might get acknowledged by the one you wait to be seen by. My easy solution is try to see why you are being accused of wrongdoing. Instead of arguing, try to see yourself through the eyes of the others.

POEM NINE:

FAITH IS MY GLOWING CANDLES

"Religious subjugation is leaving the society faithless. Yet we must have faith in ourselves as without it, you won't even believe in yourself, so how could you believe in the others?"

FAITH IS MY GLOWING CANDLES

"What is faith?" I ask myself.

Is it having faith?

Is it believing

In my religion,

In my society,

Or is it

To have faith

In my neighbors?

Or maybe it is

To have faith

In my friends.

Maybe it is

To have faith

In my family.

Or is it all of the above?

Yet then why does it feel

I am lacking in

My faith?

For everyone around me

Promises I have my faith

Wrong.

For everyone walks into

Different houses of worshipping.

My heart wants to

Hold on to all,

Yet they don't want me

Holding all

But just one.

I trust my society.

I believe my neighbors.

I trust my friends.

I have faith in

My family.

Yet then why are

Their candles

Not shimmering

And keeping my path

Glowing,

Or giving me hope?

Are they all lost

And have found different paths

To travel upon?

Or am I lost

To make sure

All come home safely

Through their different paths?

Through their glowing

Candles,

I try to see my path,

Yet then I see my reflection

Within the glittering pond

Created from my tears.

I am the only one

Not glowing

For I have turned off

My own candles,

Searching for

The candles

Of the others.

For I know I must turn

My own candles on

As

It's not the faith of the others,

Or faith in the others,

But my own faith,

And faith in myself.

For my heart knows

Everyone has their own

Faith awakened

ANN MARIE RUBY

Within themselves,

As I know my

FAITH IS MY GLOWING CANDLES.

RELIGIOUS PERSECUTION:

Life is a blessing when you must learn to believe in yourself. Religious persecution has separated all humans from their humanity. Humans discriminate against the other religion even though all religions on Earth are trying to just follow what they have been taught. Life is a long journey and through this travel, you become the follower of all travelers. Yet do you in the process forget yourself? Because then, you would be the lost traveler. No one would know you were even there as you yourself forgot yourself.

What path do you take to get to your final destination? Could you step on two boats and travel safely? Or do you jump from boat to boat as you don't want to leave anyone behind? It is true we all travel through the same tunnel of life. Yet when you within this life are searching for your destiny, you must make sure it is your destination your destiny takes you to. If you keep following the others, you will end up at their destination, not your own.

The grass always looks greener on the other side. Yet when you land on the other side, you might say but your own grass was greener. My advice to all of you is simple, trust yourself and know it is then you will find yourself. Don't wait or lean on everyone else's faith while you lose your own faith. Faith is believing in yourself first. If you love all faiths, then walk on your own grounds with belief and respect for all others. Don't become their enemy or let anyone become your enemy. For the stormy winds will come and blow out all the other candles you are trying to get light from.

Remember when the storm comes, you can hold on to your candles and protect them from burning out and keep your own candles glowing. Let your candles glow and if someone needs help, do give them light. Don't burn out their candles or don't let them burn out yours. My message is simple. Stand up on your own feet and enjoy dancing on your own. Otherwise, you will miss out on the wonderful dancing event. Don't try to lean on the others but learn to stand on your own feet.

For then you will never lose hope or lose out on the opportunities of life. Remember your faith is your glowing candles that will never fade. Let's not divide amongst religions and decide who is right and who is wrong, but let's all say in union whatever faith you believe in, it's perfect as faith is my glowing candles.

POEM TEN:

BE THE LIGHTHOUSE BY THE SEA

*"Standing by the shore,
Trying to see if you have missed
your ferry boat in the dark, only to
know your promised boat left
without you for you followed the
corrupt politicians and not your
own lighthouse."*

BE THE LIGHTHOUSE BY THE SEA

Darkness evolved around

The rough sea.

I must catch the boat of life,

Yet I could not see where

The boat floated.

The travelers all had

Their torches,

Their luggage,

Their friends,

And families.

No one gave me

A helping hand.

No candles glowed in

The dark night for me.

No hands guided me

Through the seashore.

Yet I only came

To accompany them,

My friends,

The leaders of my society,

The groups that

71

ANN MARIE RUBY

I admired.
The promises I held on to
That had guaranteed
A helping hand,
Would come down from the group
Holding on to me.
They would be there for me,
When I would fall.
They would carry me
If I could not walk.
They would guide me to my destination,
If only I would follow them.
Yet tonight as I was
Left alone
In the dark,
I realized only then,
I must find
My own path.
I must not follow all
To only get drowned
In the dark sea.
I learned my lesson
To be my own guide
For the journey is mine,

The path is mine,

The destination is also,

Only mine.

So, I must be the traveler

Who walks

On her own feet,

Not the follower of

The broken promises

Of the

Corrupt leaders.

From this mistake,

I shall be the guide

And warn all others

Not to fall prey

To the wrongful promises

Of the wrongful voices

As they promise

To give everything immortal

While they forget

They too are mortal

As when they can't

Keep their broken promises,

They will let you

Drown in the cold sea.

So, everyone,

Listen to this friend

Who wants nothing from you,

But will leave you with only

Words of caution.

I ask you all,

From today,

Don't follow the leaders blindly,

Yet

Eternally you and I and all

Must open our eyes,

And not drown after

The broken promises,

But

BE THE LIGHTHOUSE BY THE SEA.

CORRUPT POLITICIANS:

The path is yours and so is your destination. Yet as a member of this society, you like all others follow the leader. You hold on to the words of your group leaders when they promise you the whole world. They make sweet tempting promises to give you all that your heart desires.

Yet when push comes to shove, you see they are all walking ahead without you. Remember they got their needs met. I understand they left behind you the one who fulfilled their desires. Here you are left alone to fend for yourself.

So, my advice to you is don't wait to drown in the cold sea. Be alert and look around yourself. Don't talk and say what the others want you to say. Listen to the words carefully and hear them out from your inner soul. Pay attention to where you are being sent by the society by the group of people you are following blindly. For I ask how anyone could see they are dumping you in the cold dark sea waters if you were following them blindly. Learn your lessons by opening your eyes and ears to your surroundings and to yourself.

If you are searching for your own destination, then you must choose your destiny. Don't let others choose your destiny for you and then you regret you are being drowned in the cold sea. Watch your own path. Make your own path. Look out for yourself and don't fall prey to the others.

Don't say or do as politicians ask you to do. Do and say what is right. So I say, don't wait for others to show you the light. Don't follow the corrupt politicians who won't show you the light but will let go of you and will only save themselves if their boats sink. Stay on the right path. Be the guide for the future as you can be the lighthouse by the sea.

POEM ELEVEN:

MAKE YOUR DREAMS COME TRUE

"If you can dream it, then it is true you can make your dreams come true."

MAKE YOUR DREAMS COME TRUE

Visionaries are dreaming

Of their visions,

Yet why don't you

Too become a dreamer

Instead of a follower?

For how could

A society,

A group,

Or another person

Know what your

Heart and soul

Dream about?

For if nothing is thought,

Or when nothing is wondered,

Or even nothing is imagined,

Nothing shall come.

From nothing,

We only get nothing.

Yet tonight,

Don't dream of what

Others ask of you.

Don't dream of what pleases the others.

Don't dream of what is wrong,

Yet only dream of what

Feels right,

What your inner soul

Awakens for,

What your inner heart knows

Is the complete truth.

For remember, your desires are

Just that, yours,

As your dreams

Are just that,

Your dreams.

So it is your knowledge,

Your need,

Your want,

Which you only know

Can only be

Your reality.

As you stand up for yourself,

And believe in yourself,

Only then,

You too like others

Can convert all of

Your inner wishes,

Your daydreams and

Nightly ones,

Which are all just waiting

To become true.

As you know,

Forgetting all the

Other voices

Can

MAKE YOUR DREAMS COME TRUE.

BELIEVE IN DREAMS:

There is only one way in and one way out from this one life we live upon Earth. So, why don't you try to make your dreams come true? How is it we are now dreaming only what the others want us to dream about?

Who ever said there are too many singers so you can't become one? Or is it there are too many painters, so you can't become one? All the politicians are corrupt, so you can't become a good politician. These are phrases repeated by the negative minds of this society.

I believe dreams are just dreams until we make them into our reality. Your dream is your guidance through your life. No one knows when our life will end, so do we in fear stop living?

Or do we make the best of the day? So, I ask you to not be persuaded by anyone but by your dreams. The negative minds of the negative characters will always be there throughout time.

Don't be pressured by them, yet manifest to yourself your heart's desires. Tonight, say with me, "I will make it happen." All positive thinking will bring upon your life only positive effects. It's only time that you have to wait out, so do it. Now stand on your own feet and make your dreams come true.

POEM TWELVE:

BELIEVE IN KINDNESS

"Kindness is human. Kindness is found when it is given. Look no further, for kindness is hidden within yourself. Show kindness to others, and then you shall believe in kindness."

BELIEVE IN KINDNESS

I start my journey

Seeking for kindness.

Knocking on the door of all,

I walk lonely

And tired

To find kindness

I had sent away from the doors of strangers,

The doors

Of my friends,

And even my family members,

Who know the question,

Yet can't answer my question.

I only ask all,

Do you know

Where I could

Find kindness?

For I see people put

People down.

They show off their wealth

Yet don't share their gain.

They ask only questions,

Yet don't answer my questions.

Time passes by

As I watch the rivers share

Their waters.

The sky

Above us

Shares her sun's

Glowing heat

On a cool winter's day.

I watch the birds sing

Sweet songs,

Yet they don't charge me

For their free concerts.

I quench my thirst with

Oranges.

I fill my hungry stomach with

The apples

That grow wild.

Yet when I come back to my own

Society, I ask again for kindness.

No one knows where I can

Find her.

So then, I take lessons

From nature

And show all

Who come to my door,

Kindness.

I don't charge for this.

I don't turn away anyone

Who needs this.

For I answer one

And I answer all,

If you seek kindness,

Then you must

Be kind,

And you must

BELIEVE IN KINDNESS.

KINDNESS:

Kindness can't be seen or heard, nor could it be held on to like a trophy. For if your inner heart says it is missing, then you must try to get it back. This world we have landed upon during these days, we don't actually see kindness very often for it is not found in our lost and found treasure hunts.

People are all going around now trying to be mannequins in human forms. It's like we have all become computers who can do everything a human can do except feel or sense or be kind. The humans walking around are all following the leaders and are saying don't be kind and show your weaknesses.

If you are being kind and have rescued a cat from a high tree, then we would see it on our evening news. A neighbor now won't come for a cup of sugar and will probably drive miles for it because they fear for their lives by knocking at your door. Children won't play with one another in fear their parents might shoot one another if they argue like kids. Yet why do these topics make it on the evening news? I guess because kindness is missing and it has become infrequent.

I ask all of you to bring back this simple gesture of kindness. Start simple by being kind. Maybe then our society and our one world will again feel like home to you and to me. Believe in this simple truth. Today, try bringing back this one simple human trait and tomorrow you will see our world once again orbit toward a better and kinder world. It's all very simple, just believe in kindness.

POEM THIRTEEN:

BE THE HELPING HANDS ACROSS THE WORLD

"Around the globe, if you don't find any helping hands, then it is time for you to be the helping hands, for don't let the world face any friendship issues."

BE THE HELPING HANDS ACROSS THE WORLD

Around and around

The globe we go,

Searching for the perfect person,

Searching for the perfect land,

Searching for the perfect home,

The perfect family,

The perfect life.

Yet as we awaken

From our sleep,

We find ourselves

At the same

Spot,

The same place,

The same home where

We had begun our

Journey seeking

The perfect life.

Yet as we awaken,

We realize the journey

Begins

From here,

Our home,

Where we must find

What we seek

Around the globe.

For how can you find what

You seek

If you have not achieved

This in your own self?

So, I ask all of you

To stop searching

For what you seek

All around the globe

Until you have it

In yourselves first.

As today you awaken

Again from your search,

Seeking your heart's desires,

Do be the first

To acknowledge our world needs

A helping hand,

A friend,

As you

BE THE HELPING HANDS ACROSS THE WORLD.

FRIENDSHIP:

The perfect person begins with you the individual becoming an example. Be an example we have heard so many times throughout centuries. I opened my windows and doors trying to let the natural breeze flow into my home. Yet on a day that exceeds 100 degrees Fahrenheit, there were no winds, no clouds, or any sign of cooling down.

I knew I had to do something, so I turned on the ceiling fans. I had to do it myself. In life, sometimes we try to find someone who could help us and be there for us or just stand by us. Once I saw a shadow of hope come around the corner when I was lost and stranded on a dark road. I waited for a while as I kept on seeing a shadow walking toward me.

Yet after a close inspection, I realized the shadow was my own. So, I got up on my own feet and found my own way back home. It's true angels in human form are out there and they do appear during our times of need. Yet I believe if you are looking for a helping hand, then be the helping hand. Go and help others not to get back a helping hand but to teach people it's all right to offer help or just to ask for help. There is nothing wrong in being a kind and generous human or showing others you are in need of help.

Remember as you become the kind helping hand, people around you will follow your footsteps. So in the future, if a lonely person gets lost and seeks a helping hand, she will find one. The people who had followed your footsteps will grow in numbers. You have through your actions made friends across time.

People on this Earth have a hard time with friendship issues. Be the friend of all others by being your own friend first. You probably won't meet the person that had followed your footsteps for this friend of yours will awaken through your actions left behind for her to follow. She will be just like you, yet maybe after your time on Earth. Like a glowing star, however, you will know your message sent to your friends through your footsteps is being practiced by all. The signs from your footsteps say friendship is never lost as you be the helping hands across the world.

POEM FOURTEEN:

PROWLING MIDNIGHT PREDATORS

"Don't touch what is not yours, for then remember you might burn someone who will become nothing but ashes. Yet from the burnt ashes a rape victim will rise and catch the untouchable predator."

PROWLING MIDNIGHT PREDATORS

The windows are all shut closed.

The doors are locked.

Yet the sounds haunt me.

I know within this locked cubicle,

He will enter by force.

Yet where does he come from?

How does he enter

Where there is no opening?

A monstrous shadow

Enters my room,

Night after night.

He takes away

All that I am.

He robs my inner moral values.

He robbed my love.

He robbed me from my beloved,

Whom I had saved all

My love for.

He forced himself

Upon me.

Gagged and tied,

I am

In a prison

Within my own home.

Yet how do I voice

My fear to this

Unkind world

Where he is the

Face of moral values?

Yet for him, I am

The unwanted, untouchable woman

Who all shamelessly say

Had asked for it.

Yet only my closed and sealed

Room is the witness,

I am the victim

Of the

PROWLING MIDNIGHT PREDATORS.

RAPE:

Touching one another should only be through complete consent. Yet around the world even today, someone somewhere is being raped. Sometimes these predators are unknown, yet did you know even on this day we have predators who live within the same house as the victims? Yet young girls, young boys, men, or women don't say anything in fear.

Whom do these individuals go to if the predators are people they know? The protectors of these children become their predators. I ask you the protectors of these girls or boys or victims to awaken yourselves to the situation around you before placing blame games.

Keep an eye out for these victims. They go to bed safely yet awaken in the morning pregnant with their predator's children. The world today has advanced in science and technology. We have advanced in all different directions.

Yet how is it we are still dealing with or not dealing with the one thing we all know is sacred? A woman's, a girl's, a man's, or a boy's virtues. Maybe as we become aware of the situation and talk about this openly, we will not blame the victims but catch the predators. The rape victims will from now on walk forward and help us catch the prowling midnight predators.

POEM FIFTEEN:

WORK WITH ONE ANOTHER NOT AGAINST

"Happily ever after, promises are made by two yet how is it the promises are also broken by the same two as domestic violence enters as the third?"

WORK WITH ONE ANOTHER NOT AGAINST

The wedding bells ring.

The wind chimes blow

With notes of

Happily ever after.

Yet the days and the nights

Become long

And the time sits still,

Not holding on to one another,

Not through making love,

And dreaming about

One another

When not sleeping but staying awake.

Bruised and battered,

Barely able to walk,

Hiding the bruises,

Covering up the pain

From all who

Try to

Ask, seek, and knock

On the doors

Of the beloved,

Married couple.

For why do you

Protect one another,

From the outer world

If the world you live within

Has shattered

Like a broken mirror?

Why don't you take a look

At the broken mirror

And see your

Battered, bruised

Selves?

For if you still don't see the

Broken mirrors, then

Remember the promises

That you had made

Throughout the good,

And throughout the bad days.

You will forever

WORK WITH ONE ANOTHER NOT AGAINST.

DOMESTIC VIOLENCE:

Married life is a blessing. For through a blessed marriage, we the humans grow. We grow as a society and a country. The human population get their future generations. Yet within a broken marriage, we actually lose a lot more than we gain. Children growing up in a broken marriage suffer. The battered woman or man in a relationship loses her or his own self-respect.

The person you promised to take care of eternally has become your victim as you have now become the predator. Your broken promises have broken your home, your love, and your future has lost the heartbeats your heart was beating for once upon a time. I know you are trying to wake up another dawn wishing all the troubles will be gone on their own. You hope the nightmares of the previous nights will disappear on their own.

You need to know not all troubles disappear on their own. You must wake up and stand on your own feet. You fell in love and married the love of your life, yet during your journey through life, you lost one another. So, you can in union work something out and decide if you both should walk the rest of your lives together hands-in-hands, or separately.

Don't be the abuser or the abused, as once upon a time you two were the lovers. I believe even today you can decide for the one you had loved once upon a time. Violence is never to be accepted. Don't welcome domestic violence into your home as you were the one protecting the victim from all violence once upon a time. Today, do think the situation through and work with one another not against.

POEM SIXTEEN:

Child Bride

"The child bride I am and now I don't go to bed hungry, yet if I only knew, I would go to bed in pain and in shame."

CHILD BRIDE

I am a girl

Born to a world,

Where girls have no say,

For my words remain,

Within my chest.

I smile when I am sad.

I smile when I am mad.

I smile when I am scolded at.

I smile even when I am hurt.

I ask you,

How would you know

When I am happy,

Or

When I am sad?

For I have been told

Girls should

At all times only

Smile

And never show

Any other feelings.

I got excited when

I was told

ANN MARIE RUBY

I would become a bride.

I would be wearing rich clothes,

I would have expensive shoes,

I would even get to wear makeup.

Maybe after the game ends,

I would be able to

Eat rich food,

And I wouldn't be scolded at

For trying to get

Rid of my hunger,

So I wouldn't have to weep,

And hide my tears,

For my stomach

Knows not

When to not ask for food.

I would then smile not in fear,

But in joy.

Yet the day passed by quickly,

As I was brought to the house

Of an elderly man,

Who had pretended,

To be my groom,

During our make-believe

Play.

Yet now the play was over,

So, I wanted to go home

Back to my mother's lap,

Who I left home was crying,

For me.

She had said she wished I was a boy,

Yet I told her I loved being a girl,

For now I could put makeup

On like my dolls,

For my make-believe play.

I was upset what if she gets sick.

I needed to run away.

Yet it was then in one night,

I became an adult

After I was forcefully

Converted to become a bride

Of a monster.

My tears did not stop,

Nor did my pain.

For I did realize,

Going to bed hungry

Was far better than

Being in bed with a monster.

I watched the young boys

Of my age watch me,

And make fun of me

As their parents were

Making sure

Their boys would

Grow up to be

Educated adults.

I wished upon a star tonight

If only time could be reversed,

And

My life could be different.

If only I could be born

As a boy,

For then I would not have been

A

CHILD BRIDE.

CHILD BRIDE:

Child brides are still in action around the world. It is a curse for the girls, yet for some parents it's the only way out of poverty or a solution for having a girl when they wanted a boy. I always wondered how a girl was a curse to the mothers if she too was a girl. If you needed a woman to produce a son, then why is it a curse when you produce a daughter?

In a lot of countries even in this day and age, people don't see anything wrong with child brides. The society around them makes this normal. No one sees how you rob a child from the child bride. She becomes an empty shell and grows up way too fast. She misses her entire life in one night.

I know this is the financial solution for a lot of families, yet I don't see how no one sees the tears that drown the pillows of these girls. The society around us should awaken and give all children the same respect. Children should be able to live their lives happily with food in their bellies, without worrying about becoming a child bride.

I want all of you to take a look at all child brides and give them their childhoods back. If you can't, then let them grow up like the boys and have a fair chance at life and be a bride when they so want to be, not by force. Let's all in union tell our daughters you will be a bride only when you find your twin flame as your groom, for you shall not today or ever be a child bride.

POEM
SEVENTEEN:

BEFRIEND A STRANGER

"Trust issues have placed the honest ferry man in danger. Oh ferry man, don't turn away your boat for during the storm, you just might need the passenger you walk away from."

BEFRIEND A STRANGER

Cyclone-spawning force

From the roaring sea,

Oh ferry man please

Give me a lift

For I know you are on a rough,

Journey through the rough sea.

I know the stranger who calls

You from the shore

Might be your only hope,

If and when you need me.

Yet I know oh you the lonely ferry men

Decline my friendship

As you are only thinking

I will take advantage

Of you.

Yet I am the stranger

You need help from

To cross over the sea cyclone.

While you are ignoring

The calls of a stranger,

I only hope you

Don't get

Lost and stranded

Within the vast sea.

I ask you the ferry man,

Do you ever wonder,

The stranger you ignore

And leave behind to face the

Dangerous cyclone,

Might be a helping hand?

For I can stay on shore

And not

Get in the rough sea

During this cyclone.

Yet I call upon you only

To remind you

Be aware as you enter

Your

Ferry boat during the sea cyclone.

It might be hard

For you to

Maneuver your ferry

Boat all alone,

On the rough sea.

Ask your inner self,

How would you the stranger,

Row your ferry boat

All alone,

Through the rough sea cyclone?

Even though you chose

To ignore my friendship today,

I will keep an eye out

For you as I know

That's what friends are for.

Today, you see me as a stranger,

Yet tomorrow when you need me,

When you find yourself lost and stranded,

It is then,

I, the stranger,

Will still be here,

Hoping then maybe

You will learn to

BEFRIEND A STRANGER.

TRUST ISSUES:

Lost and stranded we get throughout our life. When we see at the corner a stranger is walking alone, we walk the opposite way in fear of stranger danger. We the society are facing serious trust issues.

It is absolutely all right to fear the strangers. Yet when do we know and how do we know who to trust and when? Do we face the sea cyclone all alone in fear of the strangers? Or could we trust the strangers and maybe in union get ourselves out of the dangerous situation together?

We have to at times ask for help and take help from strangers. Maybe with caution, we could slowly start trusting some people around us as we the strangers too should slowly offer our helping hands. The process must be slow and at times in groups so you will feel safe.

If you see someone who needs help, do give your helping hands, yet keep a distance and maybe have a group of friends with you. This time and year, we all have cell phones so take your phone along with you and call for help. Don't wait and risk yourself or the person who has fallen and might really be in danger.

Just remember not to be the person who walks away or the person who walks into danger. Call for help on your phone and keep a distance. Be there for the victim when help finally does arrive. Keep the caution sign on in your heart until the trust issues disappear safely. Let's be humans with humanity and safely and cautiously all befriend a stranger.

POEM EIGHTEEN:

BE A FRIEND

"The victim of violence who has no voice, the one who won't call for help, don't worry you the victim of violence. I shall free you for I will be your invisible company, your voice, for I am your friend."

BE A FRIEND

Battered, bruised,

Taken advantage of,

My friend walks

In fear,

In pain.

Heads bent in shame.

No words are heard.

No calls are made

For now she walks

Without a voice,

Or without any complaints.

She accepts her destiny

As the ruined,

Battered, bruised,

Woman.

For today she has lost

Her smiles, and her laughter

Has faded away ever so slowly.

Today, she walks alone

Not seeking anyone.

For today, she has lost

Her faith in humanity.

She has forgotten the world

Has humans with humanity.

For today, she believes

This world remembers not

A fun-loving,

Happy woman

Who once upon a time was fearless.

For today, she believes in

A world without any humanity,

A world without any love,

A world filled with women

Who were defeated

By the unjust of the world.

Yet today I walk behind her.

I follow her from far away.

I glow my torch on her path.

I place an umbrella upon her head

For today, I want

Her to know

And believe there

Are brothers like

I who shall

Be by your side

For when you do and

When you don't

Need me.

For I am the brother born not from

The same womb,

Yet I am the brother

Born upon this Mother Earth.

Believe in nothing but

My dear sister,

Believe in the sons of this world

Who are out there,

Waiting only

To protect you

And always repeat to

You and all,

We the sons, the brothers, the fathers

Of this Mother Earth,

Shall always

BE A FRIEND.

VICTIM OF VIOLENCE:

"It shall never be me." That's what all the victims will tell you when they tell you their stories. You too will repeat, "It's them and it's their problem. Never shall it touch me," until you the denier of this violent act too become a victim. Yet after becoming the victim, it will then forever be a trust issue. Who do you trust? How do you get over this violent act?

Do know it's now your turn to stand up and tell your story, the story where you became the warning sound and the guiding light for all other victims. The first step is teaching them to trust themselves first. For all the victims are like burning ashes, yet they must awaken like the rising phoenix.

It is hard to trust once you have been burned. Yet do know in this world where we have the beastly human prowling around, we have here the sons and the daughters, the brothers and the sisters, and the fathers and the mothers. I know they will at all cost protect all of us who need help. They don't need to be related to you as they are humans with humanity.

Believe in them and know our world is blessed to have them even during these dark days for the sun appears each morning after a dark night's struggle. Each day somewhere in this world, another son, another daughter is also born to be there during our times of need. I will be waiting for them and I know all of you should wait and believe in them.

Don't ever lose hope as hope never gives up on you. Battered bruises and burned by a husband, a lover, a parent, or maybe a brother, and scared of all the people around you, do know even if your own biological family rejects you, there are angels who walk around like human brothers.

Today as you awaken and greet the new dawn, do know never to give up on a true friend and maybe you can smile and be a friend.

POEM NINETEEN:

DON'T FEAR THE STORMS

"Depression, the tsunami you fear tonight, might be the confidence you will befriend tomorrow, and make you the stronger."

DON'T FEAR THE STORMS

Depression, the unseen

And untouchable storm,

Brews within

The inner soul.

It can neither be forecasted,

Nor can it be categorized,

Yet it is now looming

Around the globe

Like a cyclone,

A hurricane,

And a tsunami.

Yet this depression

Is the biggest disturbance

Growing around the globe.

For this storm

Is hunting down not

The land nor the seas,

But is looking for humans.

This storm should know

It is powerful and it is

Dangerous,

Yet we the humans are more powerful.

As we are united
And are not alone.
The lonely weather
Called depression too will fade away
As the glorious sun appears
And
The weather too changes.
As we around the globe find
Ourselves out
From this storm,
We can then
Navigate others
One by one
Out of this invisible storm,
Which no one can see,
Or hear, or touch, yet
Everyone knows,
It is there,
Traveling around the globe,
Searching for
Other lost and stranded
Victims.
Yet as recovered
From within this storm,

We the humans will become

The knowledge

And the guide

For you the future

Prey of this storm,

We call

Depression.

It is then we shall all recite

To you the lonely

Traveler battling the

Cyclone within yourself,

Not to fear

For we too have traveled,

Through this hurricane

And have a message

We want to pass on

Only to you the depressed.

Tonight, as you fear the depression storm

Brewing within you,

Tomorrow, you too like

All of us the previous victims,

Will be out of the dangers

Of the storm we all

Know is there invisibly.

So, we tell you to be brave and be strong

As you are the biggest warrior

Who shall be victorious

Always,

As you even overcome the biggest enemy

Of the human race

Called depression.

So our fellow

Travelers upon this path,

Know today

You are the warrior.

You are the victorious for

You are stronger than

All storms united.

So, today we ask all

Combatants,

DON'T FEAR THE STORMS.

DEPRESSION:

Depression is the biggest enemy of the human race for it is invisible and can't be seen or touched. Yet it is there and has been traveling at a fast rate around the world. This storm has arrived for all around the globe can feel the wind gust, can sense the pouring rain, the lightning and thunder roaring from the inner souls of their human brothers and sisters.

This is a different kind of storm. This storm is not created by Mother Nature, yet it is brewing within the inner souls of the individuals around the globe. This storm never gives up and is always on a hunt.

The victims of this storm wish this disease too could be seen by the others. If a person is in pain, they take pain killers. What does a depressed person do? My advice is to first seek help and never wait out this deadly storm. If you are sailing alone during a storm, you need to send your SOS signal for the lightkeeper to know where you are.

As you seek help, let time heal you and be patient. Be like the sea and let the storms pass by. For remember you are the warrior who has combated an invisible force on your own. You have today become the most honorable soldier in this world. Your victory will be followed by all the travelers around the globe who too are trying to find the courage you have.

Today as you become stronger than all the cyclones that caused this depression within you, go out and share your story. You will see how your story has helped so many around our one world. So today, say to all be the troopers, don't fear the storms.

POEM TWENTY:

LET THE RAIN POUR

"A mother of a gun violence victim holds tears a prisoner as they have no color and no weight. They only become thorns hurting the eyes, so it feels good to just let them go."

LET THE RAIN POUR

Teardrops falling from the skies

Are from the people

Unjustly taken away

Through the most dangerous

Weapon in existence.

I ask you the carrier

Of this weapon,

Why do you feel so proud

To take away someone

You the proud

And the ignorant,

Can never bring back?

Today, you shall face

The teardrops

Of the departed as they watch

Their left-behind

Family members

Suffer

From the unjust,

Hate crisis,

You the unjust

Human

Have just caused.

So, you and all

Humans like you

Who so proudly carry these

Weapons that take away

Brothers, sisters,

Fathers, and mothers,

Shall witness

An unnatural

Tsunami that shall come upon

You and all of your followers.

The tsunami shall come

Breaking the skies above,

Drowning all human hearts,

As one and all shall cry and say,

These are not just teardrops,

But these are colorless and weightless

Tears that shall fall

And remove our pain as they

Shall now fall

From the souls of the departed.

The skies above too shall say

With all the lost souls,

LET THE RAIN POUR.

GUN VIOLENCE:

The number of victims taken away too early by gun violence has increased and has caused the world hate crisis to become a reality. The ignorant individuals with their pride and greed have caused an unnatural tsunami across the world. Each day, we are losing someone to this deadly violence yet no one wants to see this.

I do wish tears had some colors or had some weight, then maybe these unjust people would see them. I only wonder what would happen if the people around the globe were all equally ignorant and armed. The world would then come to an end. This catastrophic storm can stop if you the human awaken yourself from being an ignorant man.

Maybe today you can go and help bury your victim. Better yet, why don't you go and buy a jug that will catch all the teardrops of a mother? Maybe then, you can hold on to the burden of your own sins. Yet you can't get all the tears in a jug for all the raindrops can't be held by a river. That's why we have floods. You the powerful ignorant man through your racial and religious hate have caused a thunderstorm around the inner souls of all mothers, fathers, and siblings who were lost because of your hate.

I ask all of you to awaken yourselves from this sleeping hate that is quietly brewing inside of you today. Remember the departed souls are not gone. They are the stars that guide us throughout the dark nights. So tonight, let's watch them and think about our own mistakes. Let's be sorry for our actions and awaken our inner humanity and say to the skies, let the rain pour.

POEM TWENTY-ONE:

AFTER LIFE THERE IS DEATH

"Inciting violence to become the great admired one also comes to an end when individuals awaken and realize after life there is death."

AFTER LIFE THERE IS DEATH

The days come to an end

As the sun sets,

Reminding all

To be aware

As everything that begins,

Must also come to an end.

Yet why is it you the violent

Create obstructions for

Others who

Don't look like,

Or believe

Like you?

Violent you are called

And you create violence

And turbulence around all

Who disagree with you.

You take life as a gift,

Yet you remind your victims

About death.

Around the world to your supporters,

And to your victims,

Your disgraceful

Voice sounds louder,

Than the voices of just

As you are the unjust.

You are the wrong and

You take all veracious

Onto the path of erroneous.

Forever, you have walked

Only for yourself

As you only see

Your own footsteps.

Yet today,

The humans around the world

Will awaken

And show

Your day too will

Come to an end.

You have begun to celebrate

Your felonious belief

Around the globe,

Yet everything that begins must end too.

So, your journey too

Will come to an end

As we tie your aberrant belief in a balloon,

And send you away

From the inner souls

Of all human beings.

I bid farewell to you

Who is known as hate,

And I remind you,

The breathing breath

Of the criminal minds,

The world will celebrate

The death of your evil lessons.

For we the humans

Have awakened with humanity

As we see the truth.

It was

You who incited violence,

You who taught hatred,

You who divided the humans,

All the while

You veiled yourself

Amongst humans,

Not showing your true face.

Yet as you lost yourself,

Buried within hate,

You forgot

Everything that begins

Must come to an end.

Your taught messages of hate

Are being erased

From the blackboard

By the new teacher

Who has entered

With a new message

As he teaches

Hate must end.

We must say our farewell

To the old messages

With new messages

As love takes birth

As we erase hate,

For the message always was

What you had forgotten,

AFTER LIFE THERE IS DEATH.

INCITING VIOLENCE:

Breathing in and out releases all negativities from the inner soul. Welcoming positive growth and rejecting negativities will provide positive growth to our society. The concept "follow the leader," however, has been trailed from the beginning of time. The popular kid in school, the popular man in business, or the rich and famous person in this world is admired by all around the world.

What happens, however, if the popular kid, the popular businessman, or the rich and famous person brews hate, division, and exclusion amongst all? Once and twice, you ignore, yet after listening to him for a while, you start to follow him and his ways. You forget your thoughts. Your words become lost as you want to be in the group, not outside of it.

Do remember, there will come a person who is stronger than lies, who is a lover not a hater, and he will stand up against all the wrong words and ways of the popular kid in the block. Truth finds its victory as everything that begins too must come to an end. We all have one life to live and in this life, if we can't speak of the truth or walk against hate, after our time the hidden truth will come out.

Honesty and truth will always be victorious even if not in one man's lifetime, maybe in another courageous man's time. How could you the divider and the brewer of hate, brew hate from beyond? You have incited violence to get your victory. Yet you too should know, everything that begins will come to an end, as after life there is death.

POEM TWENTY-TWO:

Hold Your Breath

"Time passes by as I watch Mother Earth hold her breath, yet how long does she have to hold it before we the children realize she is suffocating?"

HOLD YOUR BREATH

Standing on the seashore,

I try to take a deep breath,

Yet the polluted air makes it hard

For me to breathe clearly.

The rising sea level

Petrifies my inner soul.

I try to breathe

Some clean air,

Yet the smog from the

Actions of the humans

Cause a burning sensation

Within my eyes.

I watch dead whales and dolphins

Float upon shore

Due to the

Hasty cooking of the planet.

Oh, citizens of Earth,

Do you not see

The heat waves

And the overpowering fires

That are burning

Down our cities and towns?

Yet we stand by the shore silently,

For we know someone else is

Worrying about it.

They can save all of us,

Yet why are we the citizens not realizing

After our time passes by,

The next generation won't,

Be able to fix the problem

Because they won't be here

To fix it,

Because our ignorance

Would cause

The extinction

Of all

The future generations.

They would not even exist.

For our greed

And our ignorance,

Mother Earth

Will perish.

The humans, the animals, the trees,

All with Mother Earth will

Be no more.

Your chosen action

To not protect Mother Earth today,

Would be

The destruction

Of Mother Earth tomorrow.

For I know our actions now

Will be the only way

Tomorrow Mother Earth

Will be able to

Give our future generations

A home upon her chest.

So, I ask you all to open your eyes

And see the truth.

Let's all act now

And do our share in

Saving Mother Earth.

Otherwise,

She could ask,

If you don't believe

This catastrophic

Human destruction,

Is the only reason

Climate change is happening,

And causing

Our one Earth

To suffocate,

Then why don't you today

Go to the seashore?

Yes, you the child

Must join Mother Earth and

Do as she is doing.

Listen to her words for she is crying

As she is telling you,

She can't breathe

Because of your

Actions.

So, you should

Until you have found a solution,

HOLD YOUR BREATH.

CLIMATE CHANGE:

Climate change is not a myth but a reality we all live in. The truth is out there for all who want to see and know about it. You can ignore it and turn your back toward it, yet it won't go away.

You will find your actions will lead your neighborhood to be burned down to ashes. Your rivers will dry out as the rising sea waters will flood your land. You will see neighborhood after neighborhood will have polluted air. You will not escape this catastrophic destruction by wearing a mask or by ignoring the truth.

The friends and politicians who tell you climate change is a hoax will not be celebrating when they too will find out how hard this catastrophic disaster will affect their breathing. One thing we the humans, the animals, and the plants all have in common is we all need air to breathe. As you lose your homes to the devastating fires caused by climate change, you will realize how it feels to be homeless.

Yet what would you the predator of climate change tell your future generations when you must tell them they won't have a home left to live in as your actions have caused Mother Earth to be extinct? Wake up today and do your share in saving our one home. For I wonder, like you had told

Mother Earth will you tell your children the same and say its okay, just hold your breath.

POEM TWENTY-THREE:

WISDOM IS INVISIBLE

"You can educate yourself by going to school. Yet to gain wisdom, you must expand your knowledge and walk through life's experiences."

WISDOM IS INVISIBLE

Education expands

The mind, body, and soul.

Go out and find the golden keys

Of life,

As you educate yourselves

Through learning.

Yet remember,

The golden keys will only

Open the door to your knowledge

After you achieve wisdom.

So, today go out and

Get to know the world,

The people,

The animals,

And the nature.

For sitting in a school

Gets you knowledge

Through stored knowledge

You gain from the libraries

Of this world.

Yet you must

Get to know the

Fundamentals
Of the human understanding
Through the nature of life,
Through living a complete life.
For that's how you
Will gain knowledge
Which will advance you
To gain wisdom,
Only as you become the wise.
Yet to be the wise,
You can't just depend on
Education without wisdom,
Or wisdom without education.
For it is like
Your soul is
Missing its heartbeats.
Without human interaction,
Your education
Is not even a reliable
Source for the solutions
Of life.
Without practicing your
Learned knowledge
Through walking

Over the hurdles of life,

You will be the lost,

Not the wise.

For without the wise,

Your knowledge is

Guideless.

For you to be the wise,

You must find wisdom.

You must

Walk through your entire life.

Be the tough and fair.

Be the patient and eager

As you must solve

The hindrances of life

With your knowledge

And with your newly found

Wisdom.

You should know,

Education you can attain by

Going to a school,

Yet

You must attain wisdom

Throughout

Your life

ANN MARIE RUBY

As

WISDOM IS INVISIBLE.

WISDOM:

The old and the wise philosophers had warned us the citizens of the modern world, not to gloat in the glories of our education for the journey actually begins when we are finished going to school and start our life thereafter. The wise men who had no education still were wise as they lived life through wisdom and self-educated themselves thereafter.

Today, our generation has forgotten wisdom and only gloats in our gained knowledge from highly recognized schools. Yet a doctor who has been practicing medicine for years knows the practical experiences are far too greater than the ones sitting in a lab or school gives us.

A grocery store clerk knew exactly how much I had spent just by counting in her mind when the store had no electricity. My friend, a mathematician, was arguing with her and had said she could not know that fast and was wrong. Yet the mathematician apologized soon after as he found out he was wrong and she was correct.

She cried and told us she could not finish her college for financial reasons. Yet she has been working for a long time and knows her job very well. She has self-educated herself through life as she also finished her basic education.

I knew she was a very wise woman who taught the mathematician, it's not just education that teaches but practical life experiences we call wisdom.

Don't ignore wisdom because you should know with great education you must also gain wisdom throughout your entire life. As you gain both knowledge and wisdom, it is then the future generation of humans will all call you the wise. Don't forget to recognize knowledge and wisdom must come as partners. Knowledge is known as you get a certificate from your school, yet wisdom is invisible.

POEM TWENTY-FOUR:

TEMPLE OF LOVE

"As an adopted child, I was born not in the temple of my mother's womb, but within the temple of love."

APPLICATION FOR AD...

PERSONAL INFORMATION

TEMPLE OF LOVE

I waited in the temple

For the whole nine months

To be accepted

By my birth mother.

Yet I was discarded

From the heart

And from all inner love.

Discarded and left all alone,

To survive without

Any survival gear.

I could not protect myself

From the mosquitoes,

From the simple itches,

The pain and burning

Left behind

By the earthly

Creepy-crawlies.

I could not even hold up

My own neck

Without you,

The blessed one

God had sent just for me.

For in the midst of my dark,

Hopeless night,

I found two warm hands

Hold me gently.

Safely within her arms.

I was not cold anymore,

Nor was I hungry.

The mosquitoes did not dare

Come near me

As you held me in your heart.

You did not hold me

Within your womb for

Nine whole months,

Yet you have placed me within

Your inner soul,

Your inner heart,

As you have blanketed me

With all your love,

As you are my mother.

Today, you have shown

To this world,

You did not have to carry

Me within your womb,

To be my mother,

Nor did I have to

Come from your womb

To be your

Beloved son.

Forever we,

This fortunate son and blessed mother,

Shall prove to this world

And beyond,

Our bond is forever

And eternally

Written with our love,

As I know God had sent me

You as he could not come himself.

You are my temple,

A temple to be safe,

And be protected within.

You are my mother,

My ever beloved

TEMPLE OF LOVE.

ADOPTION:

The adopted children of this world need to know there is a mother and a father waiting for you out there. The love of a child is not bound by birth or the womb. It is the love that binds a child with their mother.

All around the world, people are adopting children. Some become irritated when they can't have a child of their own. Yet I ask you how is it the child is not your own as you brought the child home to be within your heart? The difference is you missed out on nine months of pregnancy, yet did you forget that you have held the child within your arms much longer than nine months?

I had once been to a couple's home who had adopted a child at birth. After two years, however, they had a child of their own. They from that day had always said this was their adopted son and the other one was their biological.

I did not have the courage to say anything to the parents yet I watched the toddler watch his parents as he heard what they had said. I would like to say today, however, all parents are different and have their own ways of bringing up their children. Yet if ever you do adopt a child, please hold them in your heart and never let them go.

Maybe one day, I would be able to adopt all the children you all don't want. I wish I could have the way to do so for I would hold all of you within my inner soul. My heart beats for all of the adopted children of this world. I know we have parents who too have their heartbeats sing their adopted children's name.

I do wish this world would one day remove the word adopted and say this is my child. We are connected through the temple of love.

POEM TWENTY-FIVE:

FEAR AS MY GUIDE

"Bullying is the might of the failures as standing up to a bully and walking away is the strength of the bullied."

FEAR AS MY GUIDE

Fear grips my inner gut

As I enter the school grounds.

I am not scared for myself,

Yet for my mother.

How would she survive

If I don't make it home

On this day?

For I know on the school grounds

Awaits a boy

Who would beat me up.

He would take away my lunch.

He would take away my homework.

He would ruin my clothing,

All because I come

From a wealthy family.

Yet I will not fight him.

I will not be left with him alone

As I know he is scared.

To be with me.

In the crowd.

As I fear him,

He fears my crowds.

Tough and rough he is,
Yet I know beneath all his roughness,
There is hidden
A coward who is scared,
Of my surroundings.
I kept my biggest strength alive
Within my inner chest
As I stood with my head up
And walked away from him.
I never let him come to me alone,
As I awakened all around me,
And I did not fall prey
To his bullying,
Yet I showed him how
It felt
To be a bully
As I had him
Exposed
Without being involved.
For I showed my teachers
His actions while he
Was not bullying me,
Yet bullying the others.
Today, he is a school bully.

Tomorrow, he will be a bully at work,
And then he would be
A cyber bully.
Yet before he could ruin himself,
And all others including
Myself,
I stopped a bully
On his track,
From afar,
Without exposing myself.
I exposed him,
Keeping at all times,
FEAR AS MY GUIDE.

BULLYING:

The school bullies grow powerful by bullying other children. Bullying should be eradicated from all schools completely. Remember if not eradicated, these children will grow up and become adult bullies. They will bully people at work and even become cyber bullies.

Today, I know it is dangerous to even say anything to your bully. If you find yourself in front of a bully, walk away immediately. Don't try to be fearless and try to handle it all on your own. Walk away and get an adult if you are a child. If you are the adult getting bullied, walk away and get help.

I have a simple rule of recognizing danger from safety. It's your inner fear. Fear is our God-given protection against all dangers. So if you are scared of any situation or person, it's time to put your gear on and walk away.

As a child, my father had told me when I wanted to pick a rose, I should be aware of the thorns. It's like when a flying object comes toward us, we duck because our inner fear told us to be aware there is danger around us.

So, if a bully is after you and you need to recognize if he is bullying you personally or cyber bullying you, your inner gut feeling will let you know he or she is a threat. Walk away from the bully. Expose the bully before he exposes you as the bullied from somewhere safe, far away. Remember to fear the bully, not your inner gut feelings. For fear in this aspect is your friend, so as you travel through this obstacle, repeat to yourself, "I did this as I kept fear as my guide."

POEM TWENTY-SIX:

WIPE THE TEARS OF THE HUNGRY

"Hunger makes a human fall to the ground out of weakness yet a hungry animal hunts down all around him until it finds food."

WIPE THE TEARS OF THE HUNGRY

Around the globe,

We are fighting wars.

Above the skies,

We are going to the moon.

Below the oceans,

We are chasing submarines.

Yet within our own lands,

We can't feed the hungry.

Every day, children die

As they go to bed hungry.

They never awaken

At the first sign of dawn,

Yet around our home,

We throw away

Plates of food

That never reach

The hungry children

Of this world.

The wasted food

Would not be

A work of charity,

But a fair action of
The human soul.
We the humans
Watch our human children
Suffer and die
As we are busy
Solving how to walk on the moon,
Or go under the sea,
Yet we don't hear, see, or feel
The pain of the hungry children
In this one world
We share with the hungry
And the rich,
Who are trying to discover and solve
The problems of the Universe,
Yet don't see the hungry children
Across their homes.
Come and walk with them.
Walk for them and
If you can't feed the world of hunger,
Or rid the world of hunger,
Maybe you can feed,
One at a time,
From the wasted food

You wasted and throw

Away each and every day.

Maybe today, we can help one child

Go to bed with a full belly.

Tomorrow, we shall help two,

And maybe then as you and

I continue with our journey,

We will have company,

And our growing group

Will in union feed

Some children before they go

To bed hungry tonight.

For then, tomorrow

You and I in union shall

WIPE THE TEARS OF THE HUNGRY.

WORLD HUNGER:

The world has advanced in all directions. Today, we have moved to beyond our world as we discover new planets. We travel above the skies and beyond the oceans on our leisurely travels. Yet did you notice through your travels, we have still not solved world hunger?

Maybe if the world leaders could stop fighting with one another for a popularity contest, they too could have solved these problems. The world hunger in these days should not even be an issue. Each country could feed their hungry people for free and help their parents find a job.

The world has not spared any tears on the hungry world population. If we have money to declare war and fight one another through air, water, and road, then we can travel to the hungry world population and feed them so they too have a fair chance in life.

Let's unite for all the humans across the world who are going to bed hungry. Let's not fight against one another but against world hunger. I know if we the citizens of this world unite and ask our world leaders to be involved, we will rid the world of all hunger problems.

Time is running out even as I write this poem, for I know the death toll from the world hunger victims will increase. So, let's unite tonight and let's eradicate world hunger from this world forever. For in union, let's all wipe the tears of the hungry.

POEM TWENTY-SEVEN:

AGEISM IS A CULTURAL ILLNESS

"With age, I became wise, yet I watch you the one who fears ageism more than death have become disgraceful."

AGEISM IS A CULTURAL ILLNESS

I, the traveler of life,

Walked through my life

To be the wise.

Yet where I stand,

I know I have

Much more steps to go,

Before I become the wise.

Yet I watch new travelers,

Walking toward me,

Calling me ancient.

I wonder, when did I

Become the old,

As I have so much more

Path to cover,

And so much more to do.

I wonder why you,

The new traveler,

Not far behind me,

Are so fearful to be

At the same place,

I so gracefully stand.

I realize you are not

Afraid of death.

Yet it seems you

Fear to be at the same corner,

I so sophisticatedly stand.

I know I have with me

Knowledge and wisdom,

Yet I still am traveling,

To be the wise.

Why do I see

So many travelers

Look terribly hostile,

For it seems they don't want

To move on forward,

And be where I am standing,

For they fear not the path,

Not the journey,

Nor do they fear death,

Yet they fear where I stand.

How do I teach this society,

Not to fear me,

Nor fear where I stand?

For I know you too shall

Be here soon.

Then you will see

That others are taking the same journey,

Not far behind you,

Yet as you have

Taught them well,

They too shall

Fear even you.

Let me the wise

Share with you

Lessons from where I stand

As I am not ill, and

Neither will you be

When you too stand where I

Am standing,

Yet at your own time.

A word from

I, the wise,

Shall be passed on to you,

Before it is too late,

As the people

You have taught today

Will tomorrow

From your given lessons

Be frightened of you.

So today,

Do tell the society,

This message was given to you

By a previous traveler,

Who had said,

Ageism is not an illness,

Yet within this society,

AGEISM IS A CULTURAL ILLNESS.

AGEISM:

The mirror shows the reflection of an elderly person, yet the person staring at the mirror asks, "How is it that everyone says I have aged, yet my mind, body, and soul say I have aged backward and feel young?" That's what I have written in one of my novels.

I believe you become younger as time only takes away the years. So, we start at one hundred and get younger by the day we live on Earth. Yet why does it bother everyone? I guess it does not bother them but they fear ageism.

You fear getting old yet then why do you say that you are as old as you feel? I must say you are quite the hypocrite who hides behind your fears. As people turn forty years old, the young generation start calling people old. They say the ones who have passed forty are over their prime. Yet I would like to remind you, how would you say we stop ageism?

If a person passes away young, he would forever be young. If a person lives to write more stories through her life, you call her old. I believe this is a personal illness that grips your inner fears of being older than forty.

Strange as life expectancy has increased, you want others to be old at forty. Do you understand days will pass and you too will be standing at the corner called forty? Will you then say you are old, or the society is ill and fears ageism, so they name call yourself or the others?

It's like you are the bully who fears getting old. Instead of walking with all, together through life, you become the bully. It seems the elementary school bullies have not grown up and fear growing up. So, they bully the grown-ups. Today, I would want all of you to look at life differently.

Don't fear the young or the old, but live life to the fullest. Don't fear death or getting old but give dignity to the growing population of humans who live longer. I believe you too would like to live longer with dignity. Ageism is not a disease but you the members of this society have made it so ageism is a cultural illness.

POEM TWENTY-EIGHT:

SCARCITY OF SUSTENANCE

"A powerful mount and his rider are coming slowly, yet forcefully, toward Earth. You don't see him? Yet two-thirds of the world population do see him as he is called food shortage."

SCARCITY OF SUSTENANCE

"Give us our daily bread,"

Cry two-thirds

Of humans across the world.

Yet the bread appears not

Within their hands.

The grocery store shelves

Are bare.

The prices have been hiked,

So only the rich can afford the

Inadequate foods available.

This very visible crisis

Has caused

Lack of food

Around the globe,

To feed the hungry.

Oh, all humans

Across the globe,

Recognize now,

This is a violent crime

Against humanity.

Yet why is it no one sees,

No one hears,

The forbidden question

No world leader wants to ask,

Neither would confirm

Or would dare to say,

The most feared question,

Is our world

Now facing

A food shortage?

I call for all the humans

Around the globe

To wake up today,

For we have no time to waste.

Remember my words.

This crisis has no borders

Across the one world.

This crisis will touch

Your land as

This crisis will

Spread into my land,

For this crisis keeps no boundaries.

Oh, the citizens of this world,

Let's now become friends

As we can only then

In union,

Solve this world crisis.

If only we unite,

For one and for all,

For then we can all

Even on our own foot and with our own hand

Beat the invisible

Danger that

Comes riding on his horse

To wipe the world citizens out,

Through

SCARCITY OF SUSTENANCE.

FOOD SHORTAGE:

The world food shortage is not too far away from becoming a catastrophic world crisis. This storm is galloping toward us, riding a horse. Yet we the humans ignoring this problem are all laying fast asleep. We close our doors and windows and let two-thirds of the human population deal with it. Yes, the one-third of the rich population doesn't want to worry or bother about this crisis as they will triple pay for their bread and eggs while the rest of the population go hungry.

I ask you, are you that selfish? Won't you wake up and walk out of your comfy house and at least take a look at the problem? I know rich or poor, individually we can't do anything. Yet collectively, we can do something.

I want to take the first step and admit to all, I too believe we are going to be facing a serious food shortage if we don't act now. So, now come on everyone and let's in union take a look at this problem. For with all crises, we must first find out the crisis. Then, we can in union solve the crisis. Where and when we do see and in union face a crisis, I believe we can in union find a solution.

Nothing is ever hopeless. So, today know that our world is facing a crisis that we will solve together as we unite as the humans of this one world. Do wake up and now tell your friends and neighbors, we need to solve this crisis I call scarcity of sustenance.

POEM TWENTY-NINE:

UNTIL WE MEET AGAIN

"If your heart beats no more, then why does my heart still beat? I feel like it's not you but I lost myself. Then, who am I grieving for? You or myself?"

UNTIL WE MEET AGAIN

The scorching sun

Drenches over

Where you lay asleep.

I try to lay over you,

Ever so gently

So you don't get sunburned.

The pouring rain drenches

Your bed,

Yet you don't complain.

I stand over where you sit

With an umbrella

For I know you fear

The roaring thunders

And the pouring rain.

As I look up and see a sign

Over the little ground

You lay asleep in,

It says,

Don't disturb the dead.

Yet how are you the dead

If you are sleeping so

Ever peacefully,

ANN MARIE RUBY

For I am the living dead,
As I wait for you
To come back to me.
I fell asleep
On top of where
You sleep so ever peacefully.
In my dreams, you came
To me,
Smiling and laughing
At me for missing you.
You held me ever so tightly
And asked me to
Be myself,
The ever-smiling person.
I had told you,
I know how to live.
I shall go on living
For you with your memories.
Forever you will be with me,
Through my memories.
I shall laugh,
As you loved to make me smile.
I shall enjoy life,
As you loved to enjoy

The life we shared.

For it's then you kissed my head

So ever gently and you said,

No ugly cries, no feeling lonely,

As within my heartbeats,

Your heart still beats.

To remember where you are,

You still can see me

And where I am,

I still can feel you.

It matters not if we cannot

See one another,

For we are together even

In death,

As we were in life,

Through our memories.

For you told me

To breathe and be happy

UNTIL WE MEET AGAIN.

GRIEF:

The departed can't come back. They can't be with us. That's what we were told. Yet I believe they can come back and they can be with us through memories, through words left with us. Also, if they can't come back, then when it's God's time for us to go to them, we shall. Until then, everyone smile and say until we meet again.

It's all right to grieve and let time heal the pain. Yet it's also good to know they have gone to a place where we too shall go and be with them. As I had watched my father being buried I knew I won't ever see him again. I could never ask him for advice or help. Yet I was wrong.

I came home and had a dream. I watched him happy in Heaven. He had said his pain and sufferings had all ended. Also, time and waiting is in our world. For them, it's the same day. Keep that in mind and live life happily with the memories of your departed family members or friends in your heart. When you do miss them, I am positive they will come and pay you a visit as you get them as a visitor in your dreams.

Remember everyone, grief is natural. It's our way of coping. The pain and suffering will continue because you will always miss him. Yet it will get easier as life moves on.

Keep it in your mind that life on Earth for everyone is only a day as that's what they feel, and we should learn to accept and feel the same. All days come to an end and so we shall all reunite with our loved ones. Until then, let's make this life the best life we can make it for that's how our loved one's would want us to live.

Tonight, if you are feeling the pain and it feels like this pouring rainy day will never end, I know it will end as for everyone, life on this Earth is but a day. So, smile, be happy, and remember what your beloved had said, "Until we meet again."

POEM THIRTY:

IT'S WHO I AM

"I can't be you, so there is no reason for you to pressure me to be you, for it is that I am me, not that you are me."

IT'S WHO I AM

Human expectations

Force people to go astray,

For expecting another

To be like you,

Or do as you do,

Or as you say.

You peer pressure

Humans who are lonely

And have no one to stand up with them.

You ask them to be like you,

Yet don't you see

You will then only

Make more people like you?

All around you would be

Your created mannequins.

You would only see all around you,

Individuals walking,

Talking, or acting just like you.

You wouldn't be needed anymore.

You would be invisible

Amongst them

As you would be lost

Within your own created dummies.

The world you created to be

Recognized as the great one,

Now is known

As a group,

You are lost within them.

Now you the predator

Who preyed upon people

To do and say like you,

Search for the person who had

Said to you, "No."

He is the only one standing

In the crowd recognizable,

As he is different,

For he had told you,

"I won't live to your expectations.

I have my own mind,

Therefore, I live to

My own expectations.

How I could be like you

As don't you see?

I am me, not you.

I am an individual.

IT'S WHO I AM."

PEER PRESSURE:

A child in school or an adult at work are all victims of peer pressure. No one can escape this as long as we have bullies around this world. It is you the individual who can eradicate peer pressure and all bullies who engage in this horrendous act.

Children grow up losing their own identity and want to be or dress like their peers who pressure them. Yet you can stop this at the door. Stand up for yourself.

You are an individual who can think for yourself. You can live on whatever you have and be proud of your things and achievements. The day you start acting like the bullies, you too become one of them.

Don't fall prey to these bullies. If they were so big and great, then why would they want you to be like them? They could be themselves and be proud. They want you to make them the leader and for you to not be a leader.

Each individual is on Earth to live their individual life their way on their terms, not within the expectations of the others. Don't ever give in to peer pressure, for it's the weak and people with low self-confidence who peer pressure others. You were born to be yourself, not as the other.

So, when someone peer pressures you to be like them or act as they do, or even look how they look, do let them know you were created with love just as they were. You are an individual and you have your own identity just as they do. Your fingerprint differentiates you from all, so tell them you are not who he or she is, but "It's who I am."

POEM THIRTY-ONE:

DREAM A LITTLE

"Success is the final step, yet don't forget everything begins with a dream, so why not today through the law of attraction dream a little."

DREAM A LITTLE

Live life within joy.

Surround yourself within laughter.

Forget all the pain and accept love.

Awaken yourself this dawn

To the promises of a new day.

Awaken yourself first,

Then all others

To the promises of

A better day.

All humans in union shall

Sing the songs of life

And rejoice for one another

As we in union

Learn to

Live with

Love, joy, and laughter,

For today, we again believe in humanity.

From today, let us

Not in our sleeping state,

But

During the awakening state,

Through calling the

Law of attraction,
DREAM A LITTLE.

LAW OF ATTRACTION THROUGH DREAMS:

Attract positive results by thinking positively. We can't fix the wrong we have left behind or have committed even today. Yet with our eyes and inner souls open to the inner core of humanity, truth, and just, we can fix the future, by not repeating our committed mistakes.

We can make this journey through our leap of faith in the simple truth called law of attraction. So today, let's be hopeful. I want all of you to learn from the things that have gone wrong and we can't change. Let's change the things we can change, and together let's all create a better tomorrow. Even if I or you can't do anything today, we will slowly.

Call the future to you through your inner positive law of attraction. So for the better tomorrow, today I will dream a little. I know dreams are just that a dream until we make it our reality. I know I must start from somewhere for a better tomorrow so I will start with my dreams, and in union we shall all make them our reality.

Dreams are our call to our future goals. Remember life is our destiny and let's not give up hope on life and our destiny as we can make our own destiny through dreaming and manifesting it through the law of attraction. So everyone, remember do dream about your final goal and make it your reality. Today as you lay awake, think about your future. Let's all of us make our dreams our reality as we through the law of attraction dream a little.

POEM THIRTY-TWO:

MELODIES OF HUMANITY

"Humans with humanity walk with and for one another as love for all humans ensures our victory over all hurdles. Therefore, let's cross all humanitarian crises as we understand the melodies of humanity."

MELODIES OF HUMANITY

Humanity still survives on Earth

As we are all diversified.

We have fought against discrimination.

We will overcome gun violence.

As humans object to religious subjugation,

We eradicate deadly sins, and

Protect rape victims from their predators.

Our society accepts divorce

As an individual's right to decide.

We dream about our future,

As we see the humans around us,

And learn to not ignore them,

But learn to be kind.

May we learn to be a friend and

Say no to

Domestic violence

And have support to

Say no to depression.

Let's bring back laughter

And friendship to our world.

Come and recite in union,

We will not incite violence,

As we won't accept

Corrupt politicians

Who convince all to organize violence.

They don't spare a tear for the

Child brides,

Who have their childhoods taken

Away from them.

We will eradicate

The corrupt justice systems

That don't flinch making the

Wrong into right.

We will not let any child be left alone,

And shall educate all the children

To attain their own wisdom.

Come on parents, let's

All adopt the orphans

And make sure

This world has no children

Going to bed alone,

As there are so many

Parents waiting for the children to

Arrive home.

These children will never face a bully,

Or will never be peer pressured

In their schools.

Let this world eradicate

All discrimination

As we learn how ageism

Too is discrimination.

Now as we the humans unite,

We can

Eradicate food shortages,

And never let

Another human go to bed hungry.

Let's find out where and

How the humans across this world live.

Don't stay away from your neighbors

But find out if they are grieving.

Let's tell them

Tonight, you don't have to

Grieve alone

As in union,

We, all the humans

With humanity, shall sing

And recite the

MELODIES OF HUMANITY.

MELODIES OF HUMANITY:

This poem actually talks about our one world. Here we have some of the problems we face on a day-to-day basis. Yet I want you all to know you are not alone. Never is any one of you alone as in this world, there is at least another soul going through what you are going through. Open your doors and let's find one another for comfort, security, and guidance.

Whatever your troubles are tonight, maybe my words will give you some comfort. You should know and believe it's all going to be all right. Manifest this positive vibe to your inner soul. Tomorrow, at the first sight of dawn, your problems may still be there, but eventually they will go away. We are all humans who feel, hurt, love, and sense the same way. Some of us show our feelings and some don't.

You should know we all care for one another. Sometimes we try not to get involved as we want you to get some privacy. Yet in our inner soul, our core values are all the same. We want to be safe, secure, and loved in our own place, in our own home, our own world.

All the troubles we may have kept within our inner soul as we want to be the brave. Or some of us are also being brave and are opening up and sharing our troubles. We know as one soldier comes out from the hidden doors, all will march out with courage, dignity, and honor as we all in union for our one human race sing the melodies of humanity.

CONCLUSION:

HUMANITY

"The human race living with one another and for one another equally on Earth collectively make the melodies of humanity."

MELODIES
OF HUMANITY
THE GOLDEN
KEYS

MELODIES OF HUMANITY: THE GOLDEN KEYS

Throughout time, the humans have been searching for the golden keys. They went below the Earth and above the skies searching for these golden keys. Yet they forgot within their inner soul, they carry the golden keys. If you the individual could search your inner soul right now, you would find you have the golden key to open humanity within your own soul. Then, by reciting these poems, you will be able to spread melodies of humanity around the globe. Remember within your inner soul, you have the love for all mankind as your golden key to spread this message.

Love is the temple of my soul. I find love in all humans across the world. Love awakens all humans with humanity as I believe all men and women on Earth are defined as a lover first. So keeping love as my guide, I have decided to embark upon my journey, where I will make you the individual fall in love with humanity. I believe within your inner temple, you have a bountiful amount of love hidden for all humans across the globe. My sanctuary is my belief in humans with humanity.

Keeping love as my sanctuary, I have decided to write simple poems to connect you to your humanity. Problems circulating the world are there all around us, and the solution too is there waiting for us to open the door for it. I know behind the door of solutions, humans across the world wait. Yet it is as if they are all waiting for someone to call upon them.

So today, I, the stranger, call on you to come out from hiding and join me in this humanitarian cause. There is no invitation going out as humanity is the basic trait of all humans across the globe. So today, let go of all egocentric needs and walk hand-in-hand with all humans across the globe and unite with one another for humanity.

Through this book, I have tried to let you enter my temple of love. My inner humanitarian asks you to hold my hands and let me be within your temple of love, as we in union solve these humanitarian issues. For where and when humanity is missing, there and then the human population too becomes at risk of being extinct. For I ask you the individual, how could you call yourself a human without your inner humanity?

In this book, I have written poems on different humanitarian topics. I have discussed catastrophic crises such as climate change, how we are losing our inner humanity, division between humans, diversity, rape, child marriage, domestic violence, divorce, food shortage, discrimination, depression, broken justice system, corrupt politicians, death, deadly sins, grief, dreams, human kindness, friendship, trust issues, religious divisions, gun violence, inciting violence, victims of violence, education, wisdom, and more.

All of these crises are more reasons to unite with one another. I know these issues are complicated and will need time to be solved. Yet to resolve any problem, we must first find the problem, then agree upon a solution. Then, we will see the obstacles will be removed from our life one step at a time. Yet we must act upon them now as there is nothing more important on Earth than humanity.

Time is not in our favor, yet our human values do interact with other humans and care for one another will be our strength. Our love for one another will help us in our humanitarian efforts. Throughout time, when any human needed help for any reason, he would find his human brother jumping in to give him a helping hand. I believe in the human race and I know humanity is not yet completely lost. We can bring back humanity within all humans as we show them humanity is what differentiates a human from a beast.

If you are losing hope that no one will come and help you out, don't lose hope as I know the biggest temple on this Earth is still open, the temple of your love. Through that temple, we the humans will unite and overcome all the hurdles this world is facing.

Tonight as you go to bed, remember dawn is around the corner and the bright sun will come out to greet all of us in the morning. Before you do go to bed, don't forget to open the temple of your love and keep it open with your golden keys known as humanity. For as we all open our own temples of love, we the human race will awaken humanity within us. Tomorrow will be a better day as we all awaken humanity within us. In union, we shall cross the bridge of obstacles, one step at a time.

This book of poetry is written from my inner temple of love. The human race is my first love and awakening all to find their own humanity within themselves is my sanctuary found. I hope after reading this book of poetry, you too will find your sanctuary in the melodies of humanity, and with your love for humanity, you will find within your inner soul the golden keys to do this humanitarian work.

ABOUT THE AUTHOR

"Meet Ann Marie Ruby from San Francisco, California.
This is her story."

Ann Marie Ruby was born into a diplomatic family for which she had the privilege of traveling the world. This upbringing made the whole world her one family. She never saw a country as a foreign country yet as a neighbor who was there for her as she would be there for them. After all, isn't that what families do for one another?

Ann Marie became an author as she started to place her chosen words into the pages of her diaries. She knew she must collect all her thoughts and produce them into different diaries. Each diary became her different books.

Ann Marie's life goal is not to just write something but only what she believes in. So all her thoughts and words remained within the pages of her diaries until she realized it was time she must share them with you. Otherwise, she felt selfish and knew that was not her characteristic as she lives for everyone, not just for herself.

INTERNATIONAL #1 BESTSELLING AUTHOR:

Ann Marie became an international number-one bestselling author of twenty-two books. Alongside being a full-time author, she loves to write articles on her website where she can have a better connection with all of you. Ann Marie, a dream psychic, became a blogger and a humanitarian only because she believes in you and herself as a complete, honest, and open family.

PERSONAL:

Ann Marie is an American who grew up in Brisbane, Australia. She resided in the Washington, D.C. area, later settled in Seattle, Washington, and currently lives in San Francisco, California. In her spare time when she is not writing books, she loves to meditate, pray, listen to music, cook, and write blog posts.

BESTSELLING:

Ann Marie's books have placed her on top 100 bestselling charts in various countries including the Netherlands, United States, United Kingdom, Canada, and Germany. In 2020, she became a household name as her books began to consistently rank #1 on multiple bestselling charts. *The Netherlands: Land Of My Dreams* and *Everblooming: Through The Twelve Provinces Of The Netherlands*, both became overnight number-one bestsellers in the United States.

In 2020, *The Netherlands: Land Of My Dreams* also became a bestseller in the Netherlands and Canada, consistently becoming #1 on various lists and one of the top selling books on Amazon NL. *Everblooming: Through The Twelve Provinces Of The Netherlands* became #37 on the Netherlands top 100 bestselling Amazon books chart which includes all books from all genres. Ann Marie's other books have also made various top 100 bestselling lists and received multiple accolades including *Eternal Truth: The Tunnel Of Light* which was named as one of eight thought-provoking books by women.

ROMANCE FICTION:

Ann Marie's *Kasteel Vrederic* series was written in a diary fashion. She has always kept a diary herself, so she thought her characters too could keep a diary. All of their diaries became individual books yet collectively, they are a part of a family, the Kasteel Vrederic family.

OTHER BOOKS:

All of Ann Marie's nonfiction and fiction books are available globally. You can take a look at short descriptions about the books at the end of this book.

THE NETHERLANDS:

Ann Marie revealed why many of her books revolve around the Netherlands, sharing that as a dream psychic, she had seen the historical past of a country in her dreams and was later able to place a name to the country. This is described in detail in *Spiritual Lighthouse: The Dream Diaries Of Ann Marie Ruby* and *The Netherlands: Land Of My Dreams* where she also wrote about her plans to eventually move to the Netherlands.

Ann Marie has received letters on behalf of His Majesty King Willem-Alexander and Her Majesty Queen Máxima of the Netherlands after they received her books *The Netherlands: Land Of My Dreams* and *Everblooming: Through The Twelve Provinces Of The Netherlands*. Additionally, Ann Marie has received letters on behalf of His Excellency Mark Rutte, the Prime Minister of the Netherlands for her books.

WRITING:

Ann Marie also is acclaimed globally as one of the top voices in the spiritual space, however, she is recognized for her writing abilities published across many genres namely spirituality, lifestyle, inspirational quotations, poetry, fiction, romance, history, travel, social awareness, and more. Her writing style is hailed by critics and readers alike as making readers feel as though they have made a friend.

FOLLOW THE AUTHOR:

Now as you have found her book, why don't you and Ann Marie become friends? Join her and become a part of her global family. Ann Marie shall always give you books which you will read and then find yourself as a part of her book family.

For more information about Ann Marie Ruby, any one of her books, or to read her blog posts and articles, subscribe to her website, www.annmarieruby.com.

Follow Ann Marie Ruby on Twitter, Facebook, Instagram, Threads, and Pinterest:

@TheAnnMarieRuby

BOOKS BY THE AUTHOR

INSPIRATIONAL QUOTATIONS SERIES:

This series includes four books of original quotations and one omnibus edition.

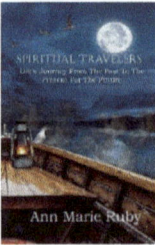

Spiritual Travelers:
Life's Journey From The Past
To The Present
For The Future

Spiritual
Messages:
From A Bottle

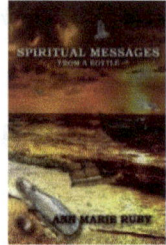

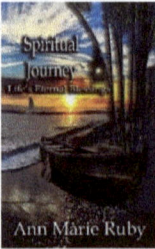

Spiritual Journey:
Life's Eternal Blessings

Spiritual
Inspirations:
Sacred Words
Of Wisdom

Omnibus edition contains all four books of original quotations.

Spiritual Ark:
The Enchanted Journey Of Timeless
Quotations

SPIRITUAL SONGS SERIES:

This series includes two original spiritual prayer books.

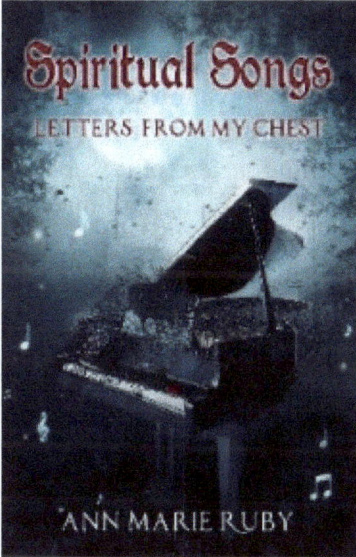

SPIRITUAL SONGS: LETTERS FROM MY CHEST

When there was no hope, I found hope within these sacred words of prayers, I but call songs. Within this book, I have for you, 100 very sacred prayers.

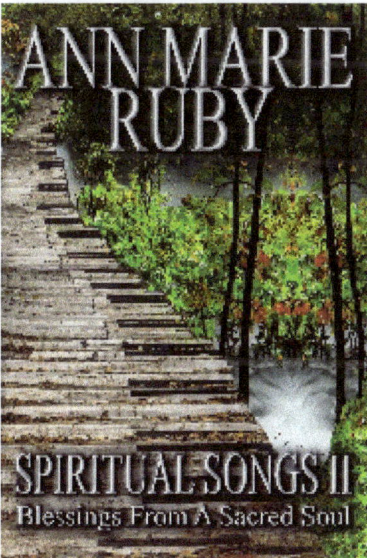

SPIRITUAL SONGS II: BLESSINGS FROM A SACRED SOUL

Prayers are but the sacred doors to an individual's enlightenment. This book has 123 prayers for all humans with humanity.

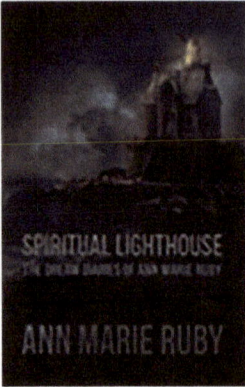

SPIRITUAL LIGHTHOUSE: THE DREAM DIARIES OF ANN MARIE RUBY

Do you believe in dreams? For within each individual dream, there is a hidden message and a miracle interlinked. Learn the spiritual, scientific, religious, and philosophical aspects of dreams. Walk with me as you travel through forty nights, through the pages of my book.

THE WORLD HATE CRISIS: THROUGH THE EYES OF A DREAM PSYCHIC

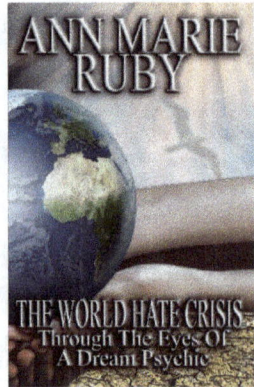

Humans have walked into an age where humanity now is being questioned as hate crimes have reached a catastrophic amount. Let us in union stop this crisis. Pick up my book and see if you too could join me in this fight.

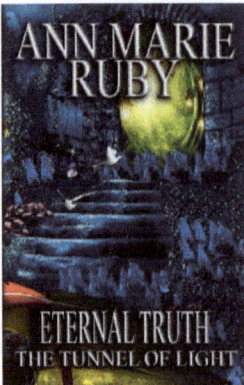

ETERNAL TRUTH: THE TUNNEL OF LIGHT

Within this book, travel with me through the doors of birth, death, reincarnation, true soulmates and twin flames, dreams, miracles, and the end of time.

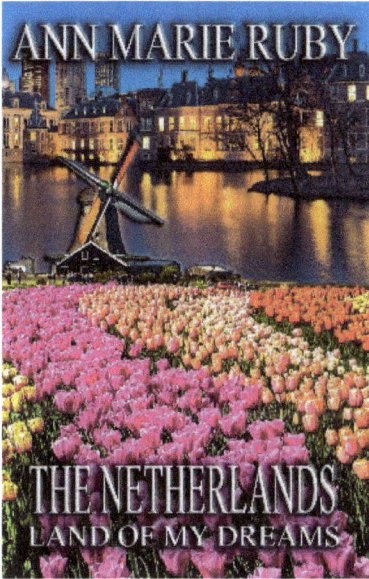

THE NETHERLANDS: LAND OF MY DREAMS

Oh the sacred travelers, be like the mystical river and journey through this blessed land through my book. Be the flying bird of wisdom and learn about a land I call, Heaven on Earth.

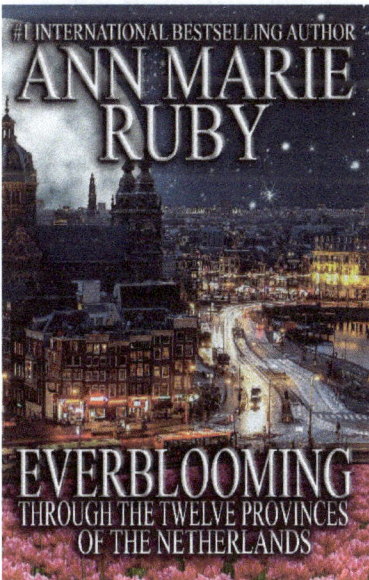

EVERBLOOMING: THROUGH THE TWELVE PROVINCES OF THE NETHERLANDS

Original poetry and hand-picked tales are bound together in this keepsake book. Come travel with me as I take you through the lives of the Dutch past.

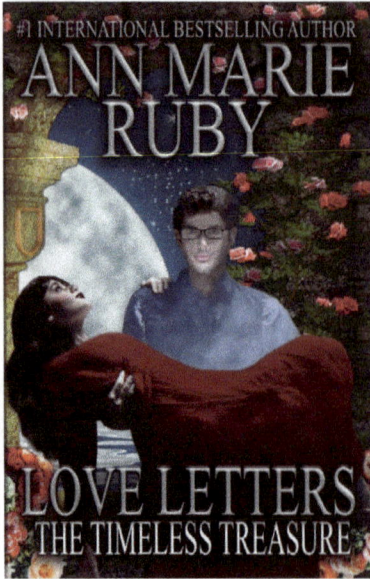

LOVE LETTERS: THE TIMELESS TREASURE

Fifty original timeless treasured love poems are presented with individual illustrations describing each poem.

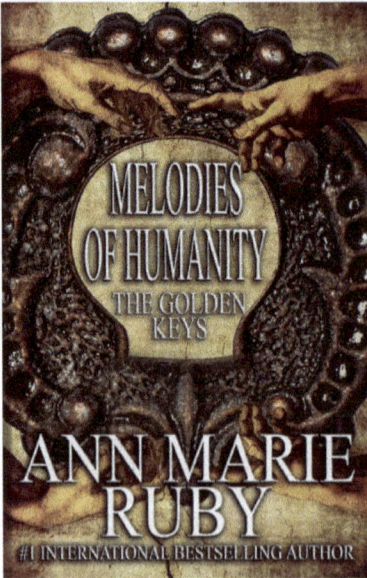

MELODIES OF HUMANITY: THE GOLDEN KEYS

Thirty-two poems retell the melodies of humanity, calling all humans to awaken their humanity through love, the golden keys everyone carries within their inner souls.

KASTEEL VREDERIC SERIES:

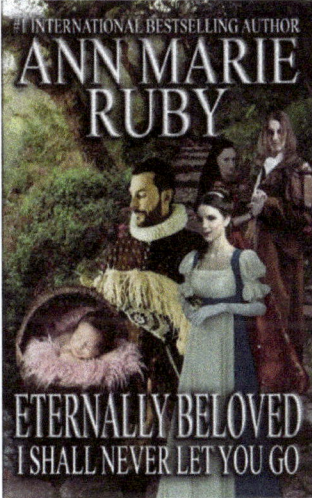

ETERNALLY BELOVED: I SHALL NEVER LET YOU GO

Travel time to the sixteenth century where Jacobus van Vrederic, a beloved lover and father, surmounts time and tide to find the vanished love of his life. On his pursuit, Jacobus discovers secrets that will alter his life evermore. He travels through the Eighty Years' War-ravaged country, the Netherlands as he takes the vow, even if separated by a breath, "Eternally beloved, I shall never let you go."

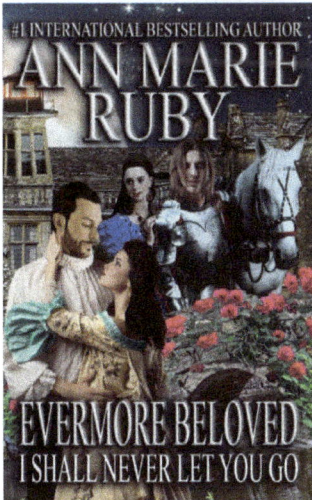

EVERMORE BELOVED: I SHALL NEVER LET YOU GO

Jacobus van Vrederic returns with the devoted spirits of Kasteel Vrederic. A knight and a seer also join him on a quest to find his lost evermore beloved. They journey through a war-ravaged country, the Netherlands, to stop another war which was brewing silently in his land, called the witch hunts. Time was his enemy as he must defeat time and tide to find his evermore beloved wife alive.

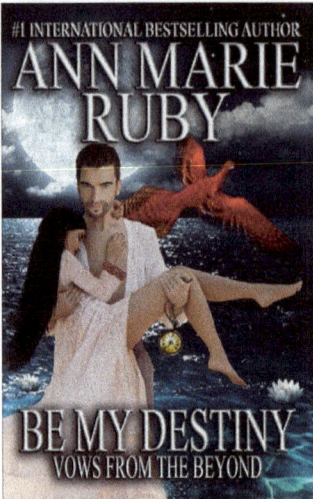

BE MY DESTINY: VOWS FROM THE BEYOND

Fighting their biggest enemy destiny, twin flames Erasmus van Phillip and Anadhi Newhouse are reborn over and over again only to lose the battle to destiny. Find out if through the helping hands of sacred spirits of the sixteenth century, these eternal twin flames are finally able to unite in the twenty-first century, as they say, "Reincarnation is a blessing if only you are mine."

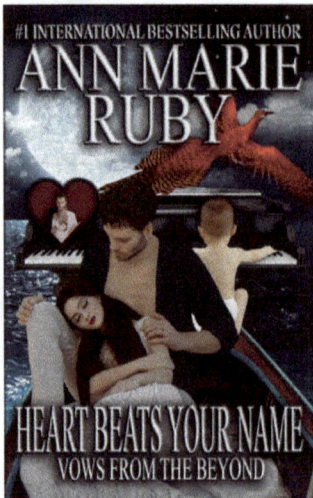

HEART BEATS YOUR NAME: VOWS FROM THE BEYOND

While one is sleepless, the other twin flame is sleeping eternally. Now how does Antonius van Phillip awaken his twin flame Katelijne Snaaijer from beyond Earth, and solve a murder mystery, she is the only witness to yet also a victim of? Find out how the musical sound of heartbeats guide him to his sleeping beloved while he solves the mystery sleepless.

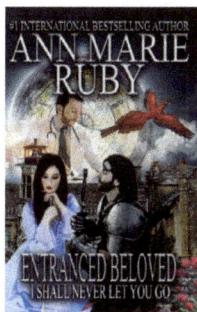

ENTRANCED BELOVED: I SHALL NEVER LET YOU GO

The pages of Margriete "Rietje" Jacobus Peters's love story from her diary slowly go missing from the library of Kasteel Vrederic. The twenty-first-century descendants fighting death and time must travel back in time to save their ancestors and their beloved Kasteel Vrederic. Traveling through the tunnel of light, the family of the twenty-first century must save the seventeenth-century twin flames. Rietje and her beloved twin flame Sir Alexander van der Bijl must create another paranormal, magical, historical, romantic diary for the dynasty to even exist.

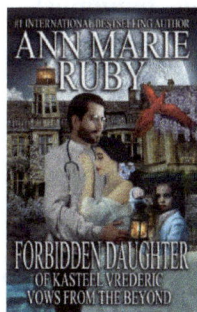

FORBIDDEN DAUGHTER OF KASTEEL VREDERIC: VOWS FROM THE BEYOND

Jacobus Vrederic van Phillip stopped pouring tears and burning himself with memories of passion to become a stone, so he could live with memories and not recreate new ones. The Vrederic family members realize the curse of past life's karma will come and meet them in this life and erase the only child who kept the dynasty going, the child known to all as the forbidden daughter of Kasteel Vrederic. The man who has sacrificed his life for all members of his family and society now must find a way to awaken his sleeping soul, recognize his twin flame, and bring back as the beloved daughter the only child he had rejected. To this world she was known as the forbidden daughter of Kasteel Vrederic.

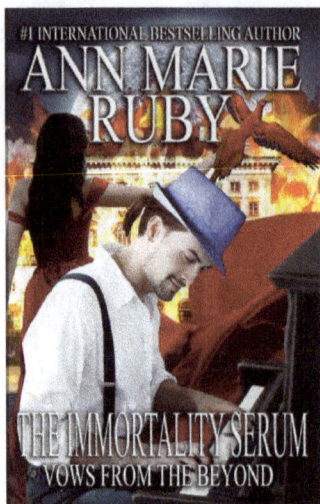

THE IMMORTALITY SERUM: VOWS FROM THE BEYOND

Andries van Phillip, the famous pianist, gets calls from his dead twin flame Tara Bella in his dreams. All dressed in red, she roams around a burning castle trying to rescue all the people from within, without realizing she was the victim, not Andries. Now the paranormal family travels across the ocean as they fight Succubus the demoness, rescue the woman in red, and solve a murder mystery, all while they know before time ends, they must find the immortality serum.

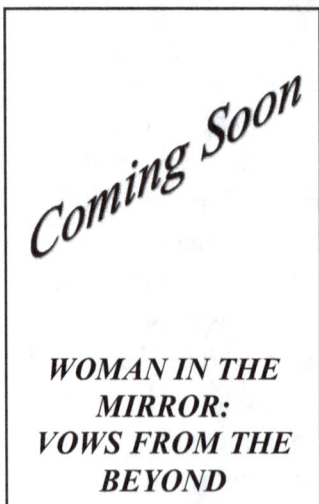

WOMAN IN THE MIRROR: VOWS FROM THE BEYOND

The eighth book in this series is coming soon.

Coming Soon

WOMAN IN THE MIRROR: VOWS FROM THE BEYOND

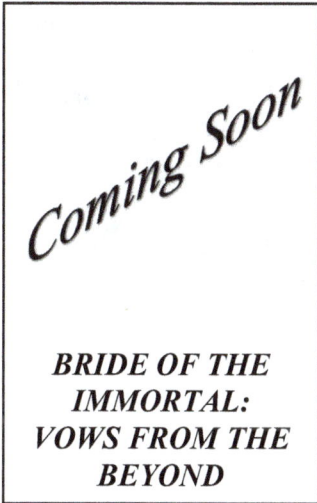

Coming Soon

BRIDE OF THE IMMORTAL: VOWS FROM THE BEYOND

BRIDE OF THE IMMORTAL: VOWS FROM THE BEYOND

The ninth book in this series is coming soon.

ENCHANTED TALES: A KASTEEL VREDERIC STORYBOOK FOR CHILDREN

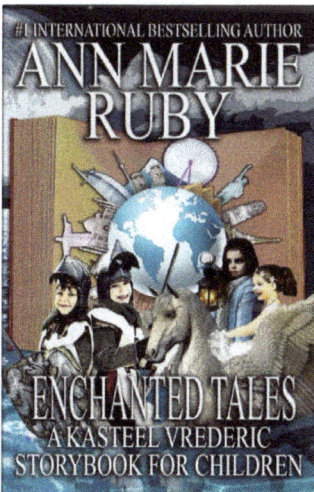

Travel around the world in seven nights. Through enchanted tales you will meet and assist superheroes from the seven continents of this world. While there, you will learn about different cultures and landmarks. Keep your magical lanterns glowing as you help the girl with the lantern solve mysteries around the globe.

251

Coming Soon

**BROTHER BEAR
AND THE FOUR
INVESTIGATORS:
A KASTEEL
VREDERIC
STORYBOOK FOR
CHILDREN**

**BROTHER BEAR AND THE
FOUR INVESTIGATORS:
A KASTEEL VREDERIC
STORYBOOK FOR
CHILDREN**

Kasteel Vrederic's second storybook is coming soon.

www.ingramcontent.com/pod-product-compliance
Lightning Source LLC
Chambersburg PA
CBHW070807270326
41927CB00010B/2325